Pers... of
Se...ty

Improving
Allied Military
Contributions

Edited by

Richard Sokolsky

Stuart Johnson

F. Stephen Larrabee

Prepared for the United States Air Force
Project AIR FORCE

RAND

Approved for public release; distribution unlimited

The research reported here was sponsored by the United States Air Force under Contract F49642-96-C-0001. Further information may be obtained from the Strategic Planning Division, Directorate of Plans, Hq USAF.

Library of Congress Cataloging-in-Publication Data

Sokolsky, Richard.
    Persian Gulf security—improving allied military contributions / Richard Sokolsky, Stuart Johnson, F. Stephen Larrabee.
      p. cm.
    "MR-1245-AF."
    Includes bibliographical references.
    ISBN 0-8330-2910-X
    1. Persian Gulf Region—Defenses. 2. United States—Military policy. 3. Europe—Military policy. I. Johnson, Stuart E., 1944– II. Larrabee, F. Stephen. III. Title.

UA832 .S65 2000
355'.0300536—dc21

                                                       00-062768

Cover design by Maritta Tapanainen

Published 2000 by RAND
1700 Main Street, P.O. Box 2138, Santa Monica, CA 90407-2138
1200 South Hayes Street, Arlington, VA 22202-5050
RAND URL: http://www.rand.org/
To order RAND documents or to obtain additional information, contact Distribution Services: Telephone: (310) 451-7002; Fax: (310) 451-6915; Internet: order@rand.org

The United States remains the guarantor of Western security interests outside Europe, and European governments are quite comfortable with this arrangement. However, Europe's dependence on the United States for dealing with threats to common interests beyond its borders cannot be sustained indefinitely. Indeed, the Senate debate over NATO enlargement offers ample evidence that pressures are mounting on Europe to play a more prominent role in defending common Western security interests.

There are political and military imperatives for Europe to shoulder greater security responsibilities outside its borders. When the United States must use military force far from its shores to defend common Western security interests, the political imperatives for doing so in a coalition with its allies will in most cases outweigh any considerations of military expediency. Under certain circumstances, moreover, a substantial allied military contribution would improve prospects for military success. Without such a contribution, a danger exists that U.S. political and public support for NATO, including further enlargement, will erode in lockstep with U.S. engagement in Europe.

The challenge that the United States confronts is therefore twofold: first, to ensure that allied governments are prepared to carry out missions that go beyond peacekeeping operations in and around Europe; and second, to ensure that allied military contributions are effective in dealing with the external threats that the Alliance is most likely to face in the future. This is especially the case in the Persian Gulf—a region in which Europe remains totally dependent on U.S.

military muscle to protect oil supplies and in which the United States and its European allies face a growing capabilities gap.

This study offers one of the first comprehensive assessments since the April 1999 NATO Summit of European countries' attitudes toward missions that go beyond peacekeeping operations in Europe. Drawing on other RAND research, it explores the conditions under which the United States would need a substantial contribution from its allies; evaluates allied power projection capabilities; and identifies key means by which the United States and its NATO allies could enhance those capabilities while improving the ability of European forces to operate effectively in military operations outside their borders. Although the study offers a sobering assessment of the political, military, and budgetary challenges NATO's European countries face, it also sets forth a strategy that is well within their reach for securing a greater allied military contribution in the Persian Gulf. Its conclusions and recommendations, moreover, are relevant to the ongoing debate over the future role of the Alliance.

This study is part of a larger project on the implications of the changing strategic environment in and around Europe for the United States and NATO. The project was sponsored by the Commander-in-Chief, U.S. Air Forces in Europe, and by the Deputy Chief of Staff for Operations, Headquarters, United States Air Force. It was conducted in the Strategy and Doctrine Program of RAND's Project AIR FORCE. This study should be useful to government officials and outside specialists concerned with U.S. national security and defense planning, particularly with respect to military operations in the Persian Gulf, and the future of NATO and U.S.-European relations.

Project AIR FORCE

Project AIR FORCE (PAF), a division of RAND, is the United States Air Force's federally funded research and development center (FFRDC) for studies and analyses. It provides the Air Force with independent analyses of policy alternatives affecting the development, employment, combat readiness, and support of current and future air and space forces. Research is performed in four programs: Aerospace Force Development; Manpower, Personnel, and Training; Resource Management; and Strategy and Doctrine.

CONTENTS

FIGURES

TABLES

SUMMARY

The United States remains the prime guarantor of Western security, especially in protecting common interests outside Europe. In the future, however, the task of sustaining this burden single-handedly is likely to become increasingly difficult for the United States for both economic and domestic political reasons. Political and military imperatives exist for having allies that are capable of bearing greater responsibility for defending common Western interests both within and outside Europe.

During the U.S. Senate's consideration of NATO enlargement, serious bipartisan concerns were raised about the growing imbalance between the security commitments and military capabilities of the United States and those of its NATO allies. In ratifying enlargement, the Senate expressed its clear sense that the United States can no longer tolerate a situation in which its European allies are incapable of responding to common threats that originate beyond Europe, such as rogue-state aggression, terrorism, the proliferation of weapons of mass destruction, and the disruption of vital resources. In addition, there may be future circumstances in which the United States finds itself heavily engaged in another conflict during a military emergency in the Persian Gulf and will thus need an important military contribution from its European partners. In such a situation, political imperatives will dictate that the United States act in concert with its allies regardless of considerations of military expediency.

Simply put, unless America's European allies take up more of the burden of defending common security interests outside Europe,

NATO's future and America's continuing engagement in Europe could be placed in jeopardy. The challenge facing the United States therefore lies in developing and implementing a vision for the Alliance that, more than just offering the prospect of U.S. and NATO involvement in European peacekeeping operations, calls for America's European allies to contribute substantively to military operations outside Europe when common Western interests are threatened. Accordingly, this study addresses three key questions: Will America's European allies be able to marshal the political will and build the military capabilities to project significant military power to help defend the Persian Gulf? How much military power can our NATO allies project today and in the future? And finally, can Europe become a more equal partner in defending common interests that go beyond peacekeeping in Europe?

Since the demise of the Soviet Union and the end of the Cold War, NATO has taken great strides in adapting its missions, organization, doctrine, and forces to the new security challenges of the post–Cold War environment. In addition to maintaining the capabilities to carry out its central mission of collective defense, the Alliance has affirmed its commitment to a new purpose that is much more relevant to the challenges the United States and its allies face today: extending security and stability in and around the Euro-Atlantic region. The Alliance has created more mobile and flexible forces and new organizations and procedures to carry out a broader range of missions to enhance European security. Several allies are making improvements in their ability to project power outside Alliance territory. Taken together, the Alliance's new Strategic Concept and the Defense Capabilities Initiative (DCI) approved at the April 1999 NATO Summit in Washington have laid the groundwork for more closely aligning NATO's power with its purposes.

Nonetheless, much work remains to be done to complete the Alliance's strategic transformation. Currently, for example, there is no consensus within NATO regarding the use of military force outside Europe to defend common Western security interests. On the contrary, most European allies eschew responsibilities beyond Europe, especially in the Persian Gulf—preferring to focus instead on improving European military capabilities for peace operations in Europe. While some progress has been made in improving power projection capabilities, such progress has been uneven at best, and prospects for future progress remain uncertain in the face of budgetary constraints and flagging political will.

At the same time, several factors will make the security of the Persian Gulf an increasingly vital issue over the coming decade. First, Europe will continue to import vast amounts of oil from the Persian Gulf to meet its energy needs. Second, Gulf oil supplies will remain vulnerable to a host of internal and external threats. Third, the U.S. military will come under increasing strain in meeting its global security commitments at a time when it is bearing most of the burden for defending common Western interests in the Gulf. America's European allies thus run the risk that a military crisis in the Gulf could create serious tensions in U.S.–European relations.

THE GULF IS THE PROBLEM

The Persian Gulf will remain the main source of Western energy supplies over the next decade. Over the next 15 years, the portion of Western Europe's total oil consumption imported from the Gulf will increase to 35 percent, compared to 14 percent for the United States. By 2010, Gulf exports will meet roughly half of all global oil-consumption needs and will become the predominant source to which the Asia-Pacific region will turn to fill its burgeoning energy demands. Consequently, the perception is likely to arise that a serious interruption of Gulf oil supplies would cause severe economic and financial dislocation as well as political and social instability in the developing world, and this in turn could generate pressure for Western military action.

By contrast, the energy resources of the Caspian Basin will make a negligible contribution to global and Western energy supplies for at least the next 10 to 15 years. The Caspian region contains no more than 2–3 percent of proven world oil reserves, and bringing Caspian oil to market poses formidable challenges. As a result, by 2010 the Caspian will account for only about 3 percent of global oil consumption—or even less if the region fails to reach its full export potential. For the foreseeable future, then, a serious disruption in Caspian oil supplies would have minimal economic and security consequences and is thus unlikely to prompt Western military intervention, particularly in light of Russian opposition.

European security perspectives—especially those of NATO's southern members—are increasingly influenced by the growing importance of natural gas exports from North Africa. Gas supplies from
that region, which continues to be buffeted by political, economic,
and social challenges, play a growing role in European Union (EU)
economic development and modernization plans. France, Spain,
and Italy import a large portion of their energy needs from the
Maghreb, and the governments and security establishments in all
three of these countries have become increasingly concerned about
the possibility that turmoil and conflict in the area might disrupt gas
supplies. Such concerns are reflected in increased military planning
and preparation on the part of these countries to cope with a potential interruption of North African energy supplies. Indeed, if
nonmilitary means were not available or effective, it is conceivable
that such a disruption could prompt some southern members of the
Alliance to assemble a European-led force and to request NATO
support for an emergency response. In such a contingency, the
United States might be asked to provide logistics, intelligence, and
command-and-control support if not to commit combat forces.

OLD AND NEW THREATS

The security of the Persian Gulf will remain a vital Western interest
for the foreseeable future. Therefore, planning for a major theater
war (MTW) in the Gulf—particularly the ability to halt a large-scale
invasion with short warning—will remain a cornerstone of U.S. defense planning. That said, winning big wars in the Gulf will present
more difficult challenges in the future. The United States' most likely
adversaries, for example, could threaten or resort to the early use of
nuclear, biological, or chemical (NBC) weapons. They may also employ other asymmetrical threats (e.g., terrorism or information warfare) to interfere with a Western military response.

Under these circumstances, the infrastructure on which the United
States relies to conduct military operations could be damaged,
hampering the introduction and buildup of U.S. forces. In addition,
the United States and its European allies could face political restric-
tions on their access to regional bases. In this situation, it would be
up to rapidly deployable air power to blunt the invasion before
strategic targets in Kuwait and northern Saudi Arabia were seized.

Accordingly, U.S. preparations to defeat large-scale aggression will be essential to sustaining deterrence, demonstrating U.S. security commitment to the Gulf states, and maintaining U.S. predominance in a vital region.

At the same time, however, the United States and its allies must be prepared to cope with a broader range of threats in the Gulf. Because of the economic and military weaknesses of both Iraq and Iran, the danger of large-scale Iraqi or Iranian military attacks against the Arab states in the Gulf remains remote for at least the next five to ten years. Indeed, during this period both countries are likely to use other means to pursue regional hegemony and to end U.S. domination of the Gulf. The two most likely options are (1) use of NBC weapons, terrorism, and subversion; and (2) limited air and missile attacks or small-scale ground incursions to achieve limited objectives (e.g., seizure of limited territory or assets).

In other words, Iraqi and Iranian nonconventional warfare and small-scale aggression—as opposed to the "big war" scenarios that continue to dominate U.S. force planning—represent the most plausible threats to Western security interests in the Gulf. Consequently, the United States and its European allies should be prepared to deal not only with the "canonical" MTW threat but also with a broader range of more plausible Iraqi and Iranian challenges.

THE GULF IN THE GULF

A wide gap currently separates U.S. and European perspectives and policies toward the Persian Gulf, notwithstanding their shared interest in secure oil supplies. NATO faces severe institutional limitations on a formal role in Gulf defense, reflecting widespread apprehension on the part of European governments and publics about becoming entangled in security commitments and military operations outside Europe. Likewise, individual allied governments—with the exception of the U.K. and France—generally have little stomach for engaging in such operations outside the Alliance framework.

The reasons for these attitudes are not difficult to understand: many European governments do not share the United States' view on the nature of Western interests in the region, the nature of the threats to those interests, and the most effective means of responding to such threats. In particular, many allied governments, believing that the United States has exaggerated the Iraqi and Iranian military threat, prefer strategies of constructive "engagement" rather than "containment" to cope with the broader security challenges posed by these states. In addition, there is still a lingering fear in Europe that the United States will embroil European countries in conflicts that do not involve threats to their vital interests.

These reservations are reinforced by political and economic constraints. European governments face strong domestic pressure to reduce spending. Thus, the use of force in the Gulf would be highly unpopular in many European countries except in cases involving clear-cut, unprovoked aggression, decisive U.S. leadership, a perception that vital Western interests are at stake, an endorsement of Western military intervention by the U.N. Security Council, and widespread international support for the deployment of Western military force. In the absence of these conditions, the United States cannot count on a large number of like-minded allies to help shoulder the burden of defending Gulf security.

The situation the United States confronts in the Gulf is therefore rich with irony: In the most challenging though unlikely scenario—large-scale Iraqi and Iranian conventional attacks—some allies will probably be willing to contribute to military operations to defend important Western interests. In the more likely but less serious contingencies, however, the United States will probably bear most or all of the military burden alone. Participation in the defense of the Gulf will be a matter of choice rather than obligation for America's European allies—and most are likely either to opt out or to commit only token forces.

EUROPEAN FORCES: ASSET OR LIABILITY?

The prevailing view among U.S. defense planners and military commanders is that while there may be sound political reasons for the allies to fight with the United States in the Gulf, America does not need European military assistance to achieve victory. Indeed, a widespread if often unstated view within American military circles is that the allies will simply get in the way and that the United States is better off going it alone. These perceptions, however, represent only half-truths—and the half that is missing is potentially significant.

According to the results of RAND computer modeling done as part of this project, if the USAF promptly deploys a large force (i.e., four or more Aerospace Expeditionary Forces [AEFs]) to a Gulf contingency, allied air contributions would be of marginal importance. If, however, the USAF is heavily engaged in an MTW elsewhere and the Gulf is the second MTW, a prompt allied deployment of one to three AEFs could prove critical in halting an Iraqi armored invasion. Moreover, NATO allies can contribute meaningfully even if they are not engaged in killing Iraqi armor. In many possible contingencies, America's European allies have specialized capabilities that could contribute significantly to Western military operations, especially in areas where U.S. forces face shortfalls or heavy demands—such as tactical reconnaissance and electronic warfare as well as airborne early warning. Because there are limits to what the allies can contribute to an MTW, the United States should encourage its allies to maintain and improve these "niche" capabilities.

More fundamentally, skeptics questioning the value of allied involvement in Gulf military operations miss a larger point: that there are strategic and political imperatives for America's European partners to fight alongside U.S. forces in defending the security of the Persian Gulf. Therefore, in the real world—as opposed to the world of modelers and planners—some allies will provide help in a Gulf war. As long as they do, they should, at a minimum, hew to the Hippocratic oath of "do no harm." Whether they will be able to fare better than that is a key issue that this report examines.

European allies face daunting obstacles to developing robust power projection capabilities. Moving significant allied forces, especially support elements, to the Gulf is a difficult problem, although it could be ameliorated with adequate access to forward basing and pre-positioning of heavy stocks in the theater of operations. Equally problematic is what the allies can do once they arrive.

Some allies—notably the U.K. and France—are making progress in developing the capability to deploy sizable forces over a long distance and to sustain these units in high-intensity combat for extended periods. But even the British and the French face serious shortcomings, and the rest of the allies are in far worse shape in developing serious expeditionary capabilities. The most glaring weaknesses are shortages of precision munitions, especially with all-weather capabilities; insufficient command-and-control systems that can be deployed in remote areas; and limited protection for forward-deployed forces against NBC attacks. Together, these limitations cast serious doubt on the military utility of European AEF operations in the Gulf.

Rectifying these deficiencies will require difficult choices that many allies may be loath to make. In some instances, increases in defense spending—or at least a halt to defense budget cuts—will be required. In other areas, European governments will need to reallocate defense resources and to restructure forces, both of which will be politically difficult in the current environment. Even more significant, most European governments and military establishments confront organizational, doctrinal, cultural, and philosophical obstacles to change.

IMPLICATIONS FOR THE UNITED STATES AND ITS ALLIES

For the foreseeable future, it is likely that the United States will for the most part have to deal on its own with key threats to common interests outside Europe. NATO as an alliance will continue to have a strong aversion to any serious military role in the Persian Gulf. Similarly, the EU, with or without a common foreign and security policy, will continue to be wary of placing its imprimatur on European military participation in missions outside Europe—and European governments, with the notable exception of the U.K. and possibly France, will be reluctant to participate heavily in military operations in the Gulf. Most European militaries, moreover, will lack the capacity to project power in any significant way and will find it difficult to participate in coalition operations far from their borders. Taken together, the expense of improving European power projection forces, the unpopularity of security commitments outside Europe, and deeply ingrained misgivings on the part of European governments toward the use of force in the Gulf will conspire to limit Europe's focus to peace operations in and around Europe. For these reasons, contingencies in the Persian Gulf are likely to involve "coalitions of the willing" rather than NATO as an alliance. For all but the most serious threats, moreover, the number of willing allies and their ability to conduct effective military operations will be limited.

Consequently, the United States—and in particular the U.S. Air Force—must be realistic about its expectations of allied military support in the Gulf and must tailor its operational plans accordingly to fit political and military realities. At the same time, the forecast for augmenting allied contributions to Gulf security is not completely gloomy. The United States and its European allies could take several steps to help ensure that Europe shoulders a larger share of the responsibility for defending common Western security interests in the Gulf. These measures include:

- **Improvements in allied force planning.** The United States and its European allies must adapt the NATO force-planning process to the needs of power projection and coalition operations. In particular, they should institutionalize a dialogue, preferably within the NATO framework but outside it, if necessary, to formulate coordinated plans for developing power projection capabilities and conducting coalition operations in the Gulf. The key tasks involved are (1) to establish new force goals that are better suited to these requirements; (2) to reach a shared understanding of the operational demands imposed by power projection missions and agreement on contingency plans for these missions; and (3) to create a mechanism for the allied forces to execute these plans. If these steps are taken, commanders will have confidence in the size, mix, and operational requirements of forces the allies are likely to make available in the full spectrum of Gulf contingencies.

- **Improvements in allied forces.** The United States should encourage allies to focus on the most serious shortcomings in their power projection postures—i.e., inadequate precision-guided munitions, command-and-control capabilities, force protection, and logistics support. Redressing some of these shortfalls—particularly improved munitions—will require an increase of less than 0.5 percent in planned procurement spending, while other deficiencies can be addressed through more efficient use of existing resources. Given the special political, military, fiscal, and geographic circumstances each country faces, however, not every ally needs to make all these changes; instead, the United States and its European allies could seek a division of labor based on task specialization and complementarity. The NATO DCI provides a good planning framework to guide this process. Based on such a strategy, some allies would concentrate on developing Revolution in Military Affairs (RMA)–type power projection capabilities, while others would focus on maintaining and improving "niche" capabilities or on providing timely and reliable access to facilities and overflight rights. In short, the United States would concentrate on what it does best, and willing allies would perform tasks at which they in turn are proficient. This would minimize the possibility of inefficient use of resources while exploiting the comparative advantages of each country.

- **Increased allied pre-positioning and presence.** If America's European allies are to make a significant contribution to Gulf defense, they must be able to deploy forces to the region *promptly* and must operate out of a well-developed infrastructure. The most cost-effective means to improve allied rapid deployment capabilities is to pre-position heavy logistics support (e.g., ordnance and fuel) in theater that would otherwise require a large amount of lift to move. In addition, facilities in the Gulf states are oriented to supporting the operational requirements of U.S. rather than allied AEFs. The United States should encourage the U.K. and France to substantially expand their forward pre-positioning of munitions stocks and to work with appropriate Gulf states to ensure that their facilities can provide the necessary support for deploying allied AEFs. In addition to the operational benefits that would result, an increased allied presence in the region would strengthen deterrence, sustain domestic support for U.S. deployments in the Gulf, and perhaps allow the United States to draw down its own presence, thereby reducing the exposure of U.S. forces to acts of terrorism and political violence.

- **Increased military-to-military dialogue.** The USAF should use its military contacts with NATO members to develop and enforce common operational practices, standards, concepts, and terminology related to coalition warfare. Such discussions could also facilitate solutions to affordability issues while addressing other barriers to improving interoperability, including differing perspectives on doctrine, objectives, and operational tradeoffs.

- **Instituting changes in military exercises.** New exercises should be designed to identify and train for commonly executed functions, especially those related to allied power projection operations. One possibility would be to conduct regular continental United States (CONUS)-based exercises in which the United States moves European ground forces or supports the deployment of an allied AEF. If necessary, the cost of such exercises could be funded out of additional European contributions to the NATO infrastructure account. Improving coalition operations in contingencies outside Europe also dictates that major allies should conduct exercises outside the NATO framework.

- **Enhancing interoperability of air forces.** The USAF will need to pay more attention to the requirements of interoperability with allied air forces. Reducing demands on interoperability will be a key element of this effort. Such measures include avoiding mixed air squadrons; having the USAF perform time-urgent and/or data-rich tasks; having allies attack only fixed or area targets and performing close air support only for their own ground forces; and scrubbing information exchange requirements. In addition, the USAF will need to work the supply side of the interoperability equation—for example, by developing allied-friendly standards for intelligence, surveillance, and reconnaissance systems and compatible secure communications, Identification Friend or Foe (IFF) systems, and security regimes. Equally important, the USAF will need to collaborate more closely with allied air forces in the planning of air tasking orders.

The above measures will facilitate an augmented allied air contribution to Gulf military operations and will improve the ability of allied and U.S. forces to conduct effective coalition operations. While some measures will face resistance on both sides of the Atlantic, they are for the most part politically sustainable, militarily feasible, and affordable. In the final analysis, however, there is no substitute for strong U.S. leadership. Unless American leaders convince their European allies that their failure to assume greater security responsibilities in the Gulf risks serious damage to the transatlantic relationship, most are unlikely to make the force improvements necessary to defend vital Western interests in the Gulf and other critical regions of the world.

ACKNOWLEDGMENTS

The authors are indebted to RAND colleague Martin Libicki for his many insights on improving allied interoperability. They would also like to thank Benjamin Zycher and Thomas Keaney for their helpful comments on earlier drafts of this manuscript and Andrew Winner, of the Institute for Foreign Policy Analysis, for his assistance in developing the scenarios presented in Chapter Two. Betsy Maloney, Barbara Eubank-Thurston, and Angela Wyatt provided important help in preparing this study.

AAR	Air-to-air refueling
AEF	Air Expeditionary Force
AEW	Airborne early warning
ALARM	Air-launched antiradiation missile
AOR	Area of responsibility
APC	Armored personnel carrier
ARRC	Allied Rapid Reaction Corps
ASTOR	Airborne stand-off radar
ATO	Air tasking order
AWACS	Airborne Warning and Control System
BGL	French laser-guided bomb
C^3	Command, control, communications
C^4ISR	Command, control, communications, computing, intelligence, surveillance, and reconnaissance
CBW	Chemical and biological warfare
CJTF	Combined Joint Task Forces
CONUS	Continental United States
CSAR	Combat search and rescue
DCI	Defense Capabilities Initiative
DM	Deutsche mark
DPQ	Defense Planning Questionnaire

EAC	Echelon above corps
ECM	Electronic countermeasures
ECR	Electronic combat and reconnaissance
EHF	Extremely high frequency
EMU	Economic and Monetary Union
ESDP	European Security and Defense Policy
EU	European Union
EUROFOR	European Force
EUROMARFOR	European Maritime Force
FAR	French Rapid Reaction Force
FBEAG	France-British Euro Air Group
FLA	Future Large Aircraft
GCC	Gulf Cooperation Council
GDP	Gross domestic product
GPS	Global Positioning System
HARM	High-Speed Antiradiation Missile
HUMINT	Human intelligence
IDS	Interdiction and strike
IFF	Identification Friend or Foe
IFOR	Implementation Force (Bosnia)
ISR	Intelligence, surveillance, and reconnaissance
JDAM	Joint Direct Attack Munition
JSTARS	Joint Surveillance Target Attack Radar System
JSOW	Joint Stand-Off Weapon
KFOR	Kosovo Peacekeeping Force
KRK	Crisis Reaction Forces (Germany)
mb/d	Million barrels per day
MCH	Mine hunters
MCM	Mine countermeasures
MEADS	Medium Extended Air Defense System

MHP	Nationalist Action Party (Turkey)
MTW	Major theater war
NAC	North Atlantic Council
NAEW	NATO Airborne Early Warning
NBC	Nuclear, biological, and chemical
OSCE	Organization for Security and Cooperation in Europe
PFP	Partnership for Peace
PGM	Precision-guided munition
PKK	Kurdistan Workers Party
QDR	Quadrennial Defense Review
R&D	Research and development
RAF	Royal Air Force
RMA	Revolution in Military Affairs
RSIP	Radar system improvement program
SAM	Surface-to-air missile
SAS	Special Air Service (U.K.)
SDR	Strategic Defence Review (U.K.)
SEAD	Suppression of Enemy Air Defenses
SFOR	Stabilization Force (Bosnia)
SSC	Small-scale contingency
STO	Survive to Operate
SWA	Southwest Asia
TADS	Target-adaptive dispenser system
UAV	Unmanned aerial vehicles
UHF	Ultrahigh frequency
UNSC	United Nations Security Council
VHF	Very high frequency
WEU	Western European Union
WMD	Weapons of mass destruction

Chapter One

INTRODUCTION

Richard Sokolsky and F. Stephen Larrabee

U.S. national security strategy declares that the United States must be able to win two major military conflicts nearly simultaneously. One of these conflicts, which forms the basis of U.S. conventional defense planning, is defense of the Persian Gulf against the threat of large-scale conventional attack. For the U.S. military and the U.S. Air Force in particular, this mission requires the ability to project significant forces to the region promptly and to sustain these forces for prolonged operations in high-intensity combat. At the same time, U.S. national security strategy postulates that in any major military operation conducted abroad, U.S. combat forces will be part of a coalition of like-minded countries. For America's European allies— who, like the United States, import large quantities of Persian Gulf oil—this mission requires robust power projection capabilities as well as political will on the part of European governments to overcome popular opposition to the use of military force outside Europe.

This book examines potential European military contributions to the security of the Persian Gulf and other energy-producing regions around Europe's periphery. It does so within the context of current U.S. military strategy and the ongoing debate within NATO over the Alliance's purpose and missions in the new millennium as well as the transatlantic dialogue on burden sharing. This focus on the military dimensions of Persian Gulf security does not, however, imply that military means are the only option available for responding to a prolonged disruption in Persian Gulf energy supplies. To the contrary, "energy security"—a term that is commonly used but rarely defined with any degree of conceptual rigor—is more than just a military issue. A number of nonmilitary measures are available to prepare Western economies to withstand energy supply disruptions, including "hedging" strategies to diversify sources of energy supplies and to accumulate oil inventories. In the event of a major energy crisis in the Persian Gulf, moreover, several different responses would be at policymakers' disposal to deal with the disruptive effects of oil price increases. These include drawing down on strategic petroleum reserves, allowing market responses to stimulate emergency energy production elsewhere, and implementing government policies to reduce oil prices.[1] Although analysis of these alternatives lies beyond the scope of this study, suffice it to say that a comprehensive assessment of energy security policy should include consideration of the cost-effectiveness of military and nonmilitary alternatives in preventing or responding to disruptions of oil supplies, given the likelihood of consequent increases in oil prices.

The United States has declared the Persian Gulf an area of vital interest and has established a security umbrella over the major oil-producing states of the Arabian Peninsula. While most of these countries are friendly toward the West, most face conventional military threats from larger hostile countries. The most serious of these threats is possible military coercion by Iraq, and the most demanding scenario would be an Iraqi invasion—or threat of invasion—against Kuwait and Saudi Arabia that would occur with little warning and could be blunted only by the rapid deployment of air power. Planning and preparing for such a contingency offers the most effective means of deterring such a threat and will therefore remain a core mission for the U.S. military in the coming years.

There are several reasons that the security of the Persian Gulf is likely to figure more prominently in U.S.-European relations in the years to come. First, Europe will continue to import large quantities of Gulf oil, and thus a prolonged disruption of Gulf oil exports could invite calls for Western military action. Second, Gulf oil supplies will for the next decade remain vulnerable to an array of threats—including

---

[1]Bill White, "Taking the Upper Hand on Oil Prices," *Washington Post*, March 30, 2000. White, former deputy secretary of energy, recommends the use of modern financial instruments to use the reserve to moderate wild swings in the price of oil resulting from reduced supplies on the world market.

conventional military aggression, attacks using weapons of mass destruction (WMD), and terrorist attacks by countries or groups hostile to Western interests. Third, the United States will continue to bear the lion's share of the risks and costs of assuring security in the Persian Gulf. Finally, there is growing dissatisfaction among members of Congress and the American public with the European contribution to Gulf security and, more broadly, with Europe's effort to limit NATO's responsibilities to peacekeeping and crisis management operations in Europe. This disenchantment has been exacerbated by the growing strains placed on U.S. forces by their expanding global military commitments, particularly peacekeeping operations in Europe.[2]

Taken together, these factors suggest that the United States' ability to continue to bear the brunt of maintaining Gulf security is becoming increasingly problematic. As a consequence, the United States has pressed its European allies to increase their power projection capabilities to encompass a full spectrum of missions both within and beyond Europe. Although some European governments have programs and plans to restructure their forces for power projection, most face domestic opposition to expanding NATO's security responsibilities beyond Europe—opposition arising primarily from political, historical, cultural, and philosophical constraints on NATO's use of force outside Europe. This apprehension is reflected in European opposition to a "global NATO."[3] European governments also balk at the cost of restructuring forces for power projection.

Transatlantic disputes over burden sharing and American concern about European power projection capabilities are at the heart of the debate over the Alliance's future role outside Europe. There is a growing recognition in NATO that threats outside Europe affect allied interests and cannot be ignored. This perception is reflected in

---

[2]See, for example, Rowan Scarborough, "Record Deployments Take Toll on Military," *Washington Times*, March 28, 2000.

[3]Karl-Heinz Kamp, "A Global Role for NATO?" *The Washington Quarterly*, Vol. 22, No. 1, Winter 1999, pp. 7–11; François Heisbourg, "New NATO, New Division of Labour," *The International Spectator*, Vol. 34, No. 2, April-June 1999, pp. 63–72; Curt Gasteyger, "Riskante Dopplerweiterung," *Frankfurter Allgemeine Zeitung*, March 9, 1999; and Joseph Fitchett, "A More United Europe Worries About Globalizing NATO," *International Herald Tribune*, December 31, 1998.

the Alliance's new Strategic Concept as well as initiatives approved at the April 1999 NATO Summit—including the Defense Capabilities Initiative (DCI), which focuses on developing improved Alliance power projection capabilities. Some allies (the U.K., France, and the Netherlands) are already moving to acquire power projection capabilities. Nonetheless, two fundamentally divergent views of the Alliance's *raison d'être* and of security threats in the post–Cold War security environment have emerged that were papered over with vague language in the Strategic Concept.

The first view, which is Euro-centric and increasingly preoccupied with ethnic conflicts in Europe, holds that NATO's primary purpose should be to preserve stability and security in Europe—and that Alliance (and European Union [EU]) military planning and preparations should therefore focus on peace support, crisis management, and humanitarian missions within Europe.[4] In keeping with this conception of the Alliance's purpose, proponents of this view welcomed the new Strategic Concept, which defines NATO's role as extending security and stability throughout the Euro-Atlantic region, as well as the EU's commitment to take on greater security responsibilities in Europe.

The second view is more outward-looking and focuses on global threats and responsibilities. It argues that the fundamental purpose of the Alliance should be the defense of common security interests against new threats and challenges, many of which—including WMD and ballistic missile proliferation and threats to critical oil supplies— emanate from beyond Europe.[5] Proponents of this view believe that NATO's transformation remains incomplete. They argue that the Alliance should attach the highest priority to improving allied power projection capabilities and the ability of European countries to operate effectively with the United States in military operations inside Europe, as well as beyond Europe's borders. Advocates of a more equal partnership between the United States and Europe also believe that NATO should make more energetic efforts to improve its coun-

---

[4]See in particular Kamp, "A Global Role for NATO?" and Gasteyger, "Riskante Dopplerweiterung."

[5]See David C. Gompert and F. Stephen Larrabee (eds.), *America and Europe, A Partnership for a New Era*, New York: Cambridge University Press, 1997.

terproliferation capabilities, including the deployment of theater ballistic missile defenses.

At the same time, there is a debate within U.S. military circles over the degree to which the United States needs its European allies for the defense of common security interests. Many U.S. defense planners are skeptical about the political will of European countries to use force outside Europe as well as the value of the military contribution these countries could make. The air campaign against Serbia during the Kosovo conflict, which was constrained in particular by European political and military limitations, could reinforce this "go it alone" mentality. Reflecting these doubts, U.S. operational and force plans essentially assume that the United States will conduct unilateral military operations in major regional contingencies, even though America's "grand strategy" embraces the concept of coalition warfare. In a similar manner, NATO does not undertake the kind of combined planning that is needed to wage effective coalition operations outside Europe.

The USAF has an important stake in the outcome of this debate. At issue is whether U.S. national military strategy and defense planning should be based on the expectation that allies will fight alongside the United States to defend vital common interests. From the USAF perspective, the degree to which it can count on a contribution from allied air forces in the Persian Gulf could have a significant bearing on its plans and military operations, both in peace and war.

APPROACH AND ORGANIZATION

This study is designed to illuminate the issues and choices that are central to these debates. It addresses several key questions:

- What are the major threats to energy supplies in important energy-producing regions?

- On which allies can the United States rely for participation in defense of the Gulf?

- What improvements would provide allied forces with the capabilities to make a meaningful contribution to protecting Gulf oil?

In Chapter Two, Richard Sokolsky and Ian Lesser present an overview of potential scenarios in key energy-producing regions that could cause a significant disruption in energy supplies. While the discussion addresses the threat of large-scale conventional aggression by hostile forces, it also highlights other threats that merit attention by the United States and its allies.

In Chapter Three, Richard Sokolsky, F. Stephen Larrabee, and Ian Lesser examine how NATO is being transformed to deal with contingencies outside Europe and the conditions under which NATO allies might join coalition operations to protect critical energy supplies. Their discussion focuses in particular on allied perspectives on the use of force outside Europe with a view toward determining whether the U.S. military should continue its current practice of planning to conduct unilateral military operations in the Persian Gulf.

In Chapter Four, John E. Peters, David Shlapak, and Timothy Liston examine current and planned allied air force projection capabilities. In particular, they assess the extent to which the allies are currently capable of prompt deployment and sustainment of air power over long distances for extended periods of time and describe plans for improving the power projection capabilities of their air forces.

In the concluding chapter, Richard Sokolsky, F. Stephen Larrabee, and Stuart Johnson discuss how the USAF can best utilize allied military contributions for operating in the Persian Gulf. Their discussion focuses on two key questions: First, what adjustments, if any, should the USAF make in organization, doctrine, planning, training, and equipment to accommodate allied forces? And second, what changes should the United States press its allies to make to improve their ability to contribute to coalition air operations in the Persian Gulf?

Chapter Two

THREATS TO WESTERN ENERGY SUPPLIES: SCENARIOS AND IMPLICATIONS

Richard Sokolsky and Ian Lesser

How much can the United States rely on the military participation of our European allies in defending the security of the Persian Gulf? What could they contribute, and what difference would this make to the success of military operations? If the United States does need the military contributions of its allies, what force improvements should we encourage them to make? This chapter presents an overview of a wide range of potential scenarios that could disrupt Western sources of energy, thereby generating pressure for a Western military response.

THE PERSIAN GULF

The relative importance of the Persian Gulf to Western security has increased in recent years and will continue to do so in the years to come. The region accounts for roughly 60 percent of the world's proven oil reserves and 30 percent of all oil that is traded globally. American and European imports of Gulf oil are, moreover, projected to increase over the next two decades: During this period, 14 percent of total oil consumption in North America will come from the Persian Gulf, up from 8 percent in 1995; for Western Europe, about 35 percent of total oil consumption will originate from the Gulf, compared to 25 percent five years ago. Of course, there is no direct relationship between dependence on oil imports to meet energy needs and vulnerability to the effects of oil supply disruptions. Many of these effects, for example, could be prevented or mitigated by advance planning and preparations for energy emergencies, government policies, and market-based adjustments.

Nonetheless, national perceptions that severe oil supply interruptions would have highly disruptive effects play a key role in shaping the national security policies of Western governments. More important, the United States has strategic and geopolitical interests in preserving the security of the Persian Gulf quite apart from the region's importance as a major oil exporter. These include the security commitments it has with several countries in the region and on its periphery, including Israel and Turkey, and the imperative of preventing the region from falling under the domination of hostile anti-Western regimes that could use their control over Gulf oil production to harm Western interests or, as has happened in the past, change governments and borders in the region.

The baseline for assessing the adequacy of Western military capabilities to preserve the security of the Persian Gulf is to examine the threat of large-scale Iraqi aggression. This threat has remained a central planning tenet for U.S. forces through the three in-depth strategic reviews of U.S. force structure—the Base Force, the Bottom-Up Review, and the Quadrennial Defense Review (QDR)—and is likely to be validated in QDR 2001.[1] There are a number of reasons for maintaining vigilance against the Iraqi threat:

- There is no sign that Saddam Hussein has abandoned his ambition to be the region's hegemon.

- Iraq retains weapons of mass destruction and could with little difficulty reconstitute its capability to threaten key Gulf states with ballistic missile attacks. The lifting of sanctions against Iraq would exacerbate these threats.

---

[1]Some military and national security experts argue that the United States should abandon its military doctrine of preparing to fight two major theater wars (MTWs) simultaneously—the so-called "two-MTW strategy." This is one of the major conclusions reached by the U.S. Commission on National Security/21st Century (also known as the Hart-Rudman Commission). Nonetheless, while some modifications may be made in this strategy, it is likely that the two-MTW structure will be maintained. See Tom Bowman, "Shift Urged on U.S. Forces," *Baltimore Sun,* April 19, 2000; Andrea Stone, "Panel Labels Two-War Strategy Outdated, *USA Today,* April 19, 2000; and Bryan Bender, "DoD Leaders to Approve Revised Long-Term Vision," *Jane's Defence Weekly,* May 10, 2000.

- Iraqi control over Gulf oil reserves and production capacity would have serious consequences for Western interests. Under these circumstances, it is possible that Saddam, ignoring economic self-interest, would use this control to punish, blackmail, or coerce the West and friendly pro-Western governments in the region. American security relationships with Gulf Arab states, the U.S. military presence in the region, and our access and influence would all be casualties of Iraqi hegemony over the region. A radicalization of the political landscape throughout the region would also be likely to occur.

- While the armed forces of Iraq have not recovered from their defeat in Desert Storm and the combined effects of sanctions and U.S./U.K. military attacks, they still enjoy superiority over Kuwaiti and Saudi forces. Twice since the conclusion of Desert Storm, Iraq has moved sizable ground forces to the Kuwaiti border to test American resolve.

The threat of an invasion of Kuwait is remote today largely because of the U.S. military deterrent in the region. However, as U.S. forces find themselves stretched increasingly thin by multiple commitments around the globe, this military posture will prove difficult to maintain. The consequences of *not* maintaining a credible deterrent to an Iraqi invasion would be serious.

While coping with the threat of large-scale Iraqi aggression is important, however, the threat to energy security in the Gulf must be seen in a broader context. Over the next decade, a number of smaller-scale crises could erupt in the Persian Gulf that would have an adverse impact on oil production or exports. These include (1) internal conflict or instability that interferes with oil production; (2) terrorist actions that damage oil production and infrastructure; and (3) limited conventional military attacks by regional states that disrupt oil operations or coerce producers into curtailing production.

Large-Scale Iraqi or Iranian Conventional Attacks

Although Iraqi and Iranian conventional military capabilities have been crippled by war, sanctions, and, at least until very recently, declining oil revenues, both countries are likely to make slow but steady progress over the next ten to fifteen years in improving their power projection capabilities. More important, both Iran and Iraq are likely to possess a limited number of nonconventional warheads as well as the means to deliver these warheads with more accurate and longer-range ballistic missiles.

Efforts by both regimes to acquire these military capabilities are driven in large measure by their desire to attain regional hegemony, eliminate U.S. influence and presence from the region, and gain influence, especially over the oil production and price policies of the Gulf Arab states. Moreover, internal weaknesses in Saudi Arabia and the other Gulf states could provide opportunities for Iranian and Iraqi adventurism. In this environment, either Iran or Iraq could decide to mount large-scale cross-border attacks on the "reactionary," pro-American regimes of Kuwait and Saudi Arabia. This case has two variants.

Desert Storm II. An Iraqi armored invasion of Kuwait could range in size from three to twelve divisions, although the nature and potential effects of such an attack are likely to differ from Desert Storm I in several fundamental ways. First and foremost, Iraq could engage in early use of nuclear, biological, and chemical (NBC) weapons to interfere with the U.S. force buildup or to dissuade the Saudis and other Gulf states from requesting or supporting U.S. military intervention. Under these circumstances, U.S. forces could face limits on access to bases in the region and might need to use other facilities for support operations. Second, Iraq could deprive the United States of time for mobilization and reinforcement, either by conducting a short-warning attack or by continuing its military drive into Saudi Arabia without interruption. In so doing, Iraq could destroy, damage, capture, or threaten critical oil infrastructure or close air and port facilities that would host U.S./Western military reinforcements.

Iranian amphibious invasion. For the foreseeable future, Iran will lack the amphibious capabilities to mount sizable military operations against its Gulf neighbors. Iran's economic problems have led to considerable reductions in defense spending and to a corresponding decline in the size, readiness, and capabilities of its armed forces. In the longer term, however, sizable Iranian amphibious attacks against Kuwait and/or Saudi Arabia, including attacks on or seizure of critical oil facilities, cannot be ruled out. Further, in carrying out such operations Iran might attempt to disrupt U.S. reinforcements by mining the Strait of Hormuz, conducting antiship missile and submarine attacks, or launching air or ballistic missile attacks against Saudi and other Gulf Cooperation Council (GCC) ports and airfields.

In these contingencies, three developments could cause a significant disruption in the flow of oil. First, the occupation or destruction of Kuwait's oil facilities could remove 3 million barrels per day (mb/d) from the market. Second, the occupation and possible destruction of some of Saudi Arabia's key oil facilities in the eastern provinces could reduce Saudi exports by as much as 8 mb/d if exports from Ras Tanura are completely cut off. Third, Iranian closure of the Strait of Hormuz could halt 85 percent of all Gulf oil exports.

The duration of the oil supply interruption in these contingencies would depend on several factors, principally the extent of damage to key oil facilities, the amount of time it would take for the United States to launch counteroffensive operations, and whether Iran or Iraq is the aggressor. It is unlikely, for example, that Iran could sustain a closure of the Strait of Hormuz for more than one week, although mine-clearing operations could take another two to three weeks before commercial shippers were assured of safe passage through the Strait. Likewise, Saudi Arabia would probably be able to restore precrisis levels of oil exports within three months and the smaller Gulf states within six months (unless WMD were used).

Limited Military Strikes

In the short to medium term, a more plausible scenario—albeit one with less serious consequences—is limited Iranian air, naval, and ground strikes in the southern Persian Gulf. Over the next decade, the West will face growing Iranian capabilities to interfere with Gulf oil supplies and to undermine the security of the Gulf states. As Michael Eisenstadt has noted in his excellent study on Iranian military power:

> The main conventional challenge from Iran . . . is in the naval arena . . . Iran could use its mines, shore-based anti-ship missiles, and submarines to disrupt maritime traffic in the Persian Gulf. . . . And though the Gulf presents a significant barrier to major acts of aggression against the southern Gulf states, Iran could conduct lim-

ited amphibious operations to seize and hold lightly defended islands or offshore oil platforms in the Gulf, or use naval special forces to disrupt oil production and maritime traffic by sabotaging harbor facilities, oil platforms and terminals, and by attacking ships in port in the lower Persian Gulf.[2]

None of this should be construed to mean, however, that an Iranian military challenge in the Gulf is imminent. On the contrary, Iran depends on freedom of navigation through the Strait of Hormuz for most of its hard-currency earnings. In addition, Iran lacks the military capabilities to challenge the United States. In fact, Iran would stand to lose a great deal from a military confrontation with the United States or an effort to close the Strait of Hormuz. In the view of most observers, while Iran might be able to temporarily halt shipping through the Strait, it would be unable to sustain a blockage for any length of time. Nonetheless, Iran's buildup is designed to bolster the credibility of Iranian threats to freedom of navigation. Further, there are circumstances in which Iran might be likely to take greater risks to halt oil traffic in the Gulf—for example, if Tehran perceived that Iran's survival or other vital interests were at stake. In short, the Iranian threat to the Strait of Hormuz lies not in the denial of access to energy resources per se; given Iran's capabilities, the longer-term effects of its action and the overall effect on supply should be minimal. Rather, Iran's intent is to manipulate the threat to gain additional leverage to enhance its broader political ambitions in the region.[3]

One particularly dangerous contingency is a severely weakened and increasingly desperate Iran that lashes out at the Gulf states for their support of U.S. policies aimed, in Iran's view, at overthrowing the Iranian regime. Under these circumstances, where Iran might be willing to take greater risks, Tehran could try to create serious operational problems for U.S. forces by (1) conducting intense air and naval attacks with little or no warning and halting operations within 48 hours; (2) withholding the use of NBC weapons and sparing Gulf state populations from attacks; and (3) providing sanctuary to one or

---

[2]Michael Eisenstadt, *Iranian Military Power: Capabilities and Intentions*, Washington, D.C.: The Washington Institute for Near East Policy, 1996, p. xvii.
[3]Ibid.

more Gulf states. If this were to happen, Iran could inflict significant damage before U.S. forces could mobilize an effective response. By sparing cities in the initial attack, refraining from WMD attacks, and providing sanctuary, many of the Gulf states—including those that were victims of the Iranian attack—would have a strong incentive to deny access to Western forces.

The impact of such an attack on oil supplies would depend primarily on the extent of damage inflicted on critical targets, such as pumping stations and oil-loading terminals. The deployment of additional U.S. forces to the region could calm the jittery nerves of shippers, and insurance rates would likely return to normal within several days. Hence, tanker traffic would resume quickly to any ports that were not attacked. However, it could take several months or perhaps longer to repair damage to high-value oil/gas targets in Saudi Arabia. As noted previously, for example, if Ras Tanura were put out of commission, several million barrels of oil per day would be lost to the market until full operations were resumed. Under these conditions, the Saudis and other Gulf states might want the United States to maintain their augmented forces in the region until repair operations were completed.

Nonconventional Attacks

The regimes in both Baghdad and Tehran attach very high priority to acquiring the capability to deliver WMD with ballistic missiles. Over the next decade, both countries are thus likely to pursue programs to extend the range and improve the accuracy of these missiles. They will then possess the capability to hold critical oil-related installations at risk. External attacks using weapons of mass destruction could result from Iranian or Iraqi attempts to punish or coerce Saudi Arabia or to expel the U.S. military presence from the region. It is also possible, moreover, that domestic opposition groups could carry out terrorist attacks employing WMD in support of Iranian or Iraqi conventional military operations.

In all likelihood, the use of WMD would be concentrated in eastern Saudi Arabia, where most of the Kingdom's major oil production and processing/exporting facilities are located. Disruption would be caused by (1) destruction of facilities and materials, including pipelines, refineries, storage tanks, export terminals (e.g., Ras

Tanura), and lines of communication/transportation; (2) contamination of materials and structures; and (3) the death or incapacitation of critical oil-industry personnel, widespread panic among such personnel, and the exodus of foreign workers from the country.

In this scenario, oil production would plummet dramatically and the ensuing chaos and economic deprivation would put severe strain on the Saudi government. The Saudis would no doubt make a concerted effort to repair damaged facilities and to restore preattack production levels as quickly as possible; however, the extent of the destruction and the threat of further attacks by terrorist groups could impede recovery. For example, if a nuclear blast destroyed the Ras Tanura complex, a minimum of 6 mb/d of export capacity could be removed from the market, and the entire Saudi oil production capability could be wiped out if large areas were contaminated by radioactive fallout. Even if the Saudis could restore a sense of calm, it could well take years before production and exports were restored to normal levels.

Terrorism and Subversion

Both Iran and, to a lesser extent, Iraq could also attempt to use subversion, political violence, or covert attacks (e.g., terrorism and sabotage) to coerce Gulf states into accepting their political, economic, and security demands. Such a campaign of intimidation could be carried out directly by Iran or Iraq or indirectly through use of domestic surrogates.[4]

Control over oil revenues would be the major motivation for an Iranian or Iraqi campaign to intimidate the Gulf states.[5] In the future, both countries will share a common interest in driving up oil prices, especially when Iraq makes a full return to the oil market.

---

[4]Turkey is also an important conduit for Gulf oil shipments by pipeline to the Mediterranean. There have been attacks by the Kurdistan Workers Party (PKK) on these lines in the past and there could be more in the future, raising the risk not only to Gulf oil but also to oil from the Caspian if the Baku-Ceyhan pipeline is built.

[5]See Graham E. Fuller and Bruce Pirnie, *Iran: Destabilizing Potential in the Persian Gulf*, RAND, MR-793-OSD, 1996, pp. 71–74.

To intimidate the Gulf states, both countries could conduct covert attacks against vulnerable littoral oil facilities or resort to subversion, assassination, and political violence. Iran in particular has long-standing ties to terrorist cells in the Gulf and, unlike Iraq, has been fairly sophisticated in manipulating extremist Islamic movements to further its own ends. Together, a successful effort to curb Gulf state oil production and attacks on oil facilities could reduce oil supplies on the global market. Over time, however, the market would adjust to lower production/exports and higher prices, and thus the effects of a sudden and substantial price increase, while especially serious for the developing world, are likely to be short-lived.

Internal Political Crisis in Saudi Arabia

Over the next decade, Saudi Arabia could become increasingly vulnerable to domestic unrest and perhaps civil strife. The Royal Family is beset by a host of political, social, and economic challenges that have triggered growing public disaffection—including rapid population growth, corruption, glaring economic disparities, lack of political accountability, and a dizzying pace of social and cultural change. Saudi rulers have shown little interest in political and economic reforms that over the long run might address these grievances.

As a result, many commentators have observed that the Saudi government faces a widening gap between popular expectations of improved living standards and its ability to guarantee these conditions for the mass of the Saudi population. If the Royal Family fails to close this gap, it could place at risk the "social compact" that has brought political and social harmony to the Kingdom in the modern era: Government largesse to provide increasing wealth and world-class social services to Saudi citizens in return for their loyalty and support.[6]

---

[6]On changing sources of risk and the internal problems facing Gulf monarchies, see Graham Fuller and Ian Lesser, "Persian Gulf Myths," *Foreign Affairs*, Vol. 76, No. 3, May-June 1997. For a detailed discussion of the political, economic, and social factors affecting the internal stability of the Gulf states, see Daniel L. Byman and Jerrold D. Green, *Political Violence and Stability in the States of the Northern Persian Gulf*, RAND MR-1021-OSD, 1999.

If political, economic, and social conditions in Saudi Arabia were to deteriorate dramatically, a combination of developments could precipitate a major challenge to the rule of the Saudi Royal Family, an internal insurrection, and possibly an Islamist seizure of power. These include a violent power struggle over succession; the implosion of the Saudi armed forces; a challenge to the legitimacy of the al-Saud family by religious extremists; and a Shi'ite revolt in Saudi Arabia's eastern province.[7]

A prolonged interruption in the flow of Saudi oil would have severe consequences for the United States and the global economy, particularly if emergency oil production elsewhere could not be brought on line quickly. Moreover, it is unlikely that Saudi oil production would remain immune to the effects of an internal war. The oil fields themselves—or the small number of critical and vulnerable processing sites—could suffer severe damage that could take months or even longer to repair if nonconventional weapons were used. Further, many skilled foreign workers, who are critical to Saudi oil production and the target of domestic resentment, could flee the country if the war unleashes a torrent of anti-Western or anti-American feelings. Together, these developments could slash oil production dramatically.

A Second Iran-Iraq War

Iran and Iraq have not abandoned pretensions to regional domination, and their competition for power and influence is exacerbated by deep-seated mistrust as well as by historical, ideological, and religious differences. Over the next decade, a number of internal developments in Iran or Iraq could thus precipitate a second Iran-Iraq military confrontation. Of these, the chief possibilities are (1) Iranian military intervention in an Iraqi civil war that threatens the dismemberment of the country along ethnic and sectarian lines; (2) fragmentation or large-scale unrest in Iran that tempts Iraq to conduct military operations against Iran, either to contain the spread of internal Iranian conflict or for territorial or political aggrandizement; and (3) the resurgence of a militarily powerful and revanchist Iraq bent on

---

[7]See Stephen R. David, "Saving America from the Coming Civil Wars," *Foreign Affairs*, Vol. 78, No. 1, January-February 1999, p. 109.

reclaiming what Baghdad sees as its rightful status as the predominant regional power.

A second Iran-Iraq war could cause a major disruption in oil supplies. Iraq's production could come to a complete halt, for example, if Iran gained control of the Shatt-al Arab waterway, a Kurdish rebellion in the north closed the Kirkuk-Ceyhan pipeline, and Syria closed pipelines connecting Kirkuk to terminals in Syria and Lebanon. If this were to happen, 3 mb/d would be removed from the market. In addition, Iranian mining, artillery, missile, and submarine attacks on shipping and on Gulf state oil facilities, carried out in retaliation for their support of Iraq, could disrupt Gulf Arab oil exports. Under worst-case circumstances, GCC oil production could decline by as much as 5 mb/d during the first few months of the war. Within several months, however, production and exports could return to prewar levels except at the most severely damaged facilities. Given the damage to oil production and export facilities in the Gulf, Iran, and Iraq, it could take up to two years to restore oil production to prewar levels in all these countries. However, if Saudi oil facilities are spared extensive damage in the war, increased Saudi oil production could return total Gulf oil production to prewar levels after six months.[8]

Israeli-Iranian Military Confrontation

Finally, it is not difficult to imagine circumstances over the next decade that could trigger an escalatory spiral of Israeli-Iranian military attacks resulting in significant disruption in Iranian oil exports and a closure of the Strait of Hormuz. For example, Israel could decide to launch a preemptive strike against Iranian NBC and missile facilities. In retaliation, Iran might sponsor terrorist attacks against Israel, precipitating an Israeli military strike on Iran's export terminals at Kharg Island and Ganaveh. To bring maximum international pressure to bear on Israel, Iran might threaten to close the Strait of Hormuz, which would effectively shut it down owing to skyrocketing

---

[8]We are not predicting that a second Iran-Iraq war would trigger a major decline in Gulf oil supplies but are simply noting it as a possibility. In this regard, it is important to remember that despite fears and concerted attacks on energy infrastructure during the "first" Iran-Iraq war, there was little effect on energy production or access. The infrastructure and, after an initial scare, the market proved resilient.

insurance rates for tankers, until Israel halts its attacks and agrees to negotiate a cease-fire.

As a result of Israeli military actions, Iran could suffer a serious disruption in oil exports. Tanker loadings at Kharg would likely come to a halt as a result of Israeli mining of the site and Iran's shortcomings in demining capabilities. In addition to mining, export operations at Kharg and the Ganaveh oil terminals would be crippled as a result of Israeli air attacks and special operations, and Israeli mining could impede repair work. In this situation, 1–2 mb/d of Iranian oil could be lost for up to one year.

THE CASPIAN BASIN

The development of energy resources in the Caspian Basin has sparked heightened interest in the region among some NATO allies. Turkey in particular has sought to carve out a larger role for itself in the region, given its growing energy needs as well as its long-standing historical, cultural, and ethnic ties to the largely Turkic population in the area. Ankara has cultivated its ties with key oil-producing states, especially Azerbaijan, and has a growing military and security relationship with Georgia, whose location along major oil pipeline routes makes it a key player in the pipeline politics of the region. Ankara plays a pivotal role in the construction of the Baku-Ceyhan pipeline, which Turkey along with the United States and others is pushing as the major outlet for the bulk of Azeri long-term oil exports.

 Other European allies, while concerned about the potential for conflict and instability in the Caspian region and Central Asia, are more wary of deepening the Alliance's involvement in the region. Although some support efforts to expand cooperation among regional states, especially in dealing with illegal trafficking of arms and drugs, allied support for expanding NATO's Partnership for Peace (PFP) program and other military-to-military contacts has been lukewarm at best. NATO allies have shown no interest, moreover, in considering any of the Central Asian or Caspian countries for participation in the Alliance's Membership Action Plan. In addition, none of the European allies shares Turkey's interest in protecting oil pipelines in the region.

The arm's-length attitude of most NATO allies toward the region reflects in large measure their desire to avoid antagonizing Russia. To some degree it also reflects a recognition that Caspian energy supplies will not make a significant contribution to the diversification of European energy supplies for the foreseeable future, given the numerous political, geographic, economic, and technical constraints on Caspian energy development. Indeed, the Caspian Basin by most projections is expected to export no more than 2–3 mb/d by 2010, thereby meeting only 2–3 percent of global energy demand—prompting one prominent energy analyst to conclude that while Caspian oil could play an important role at the margin by diversifying energy supplies, its role will not be pivotal.[9] In contrast to the Persian Gulf, it is therefore unlikely that Caspian energy supplies will be disrupted over the next decade as a result of conventional military actions by regional states or decisions by national governments to reduce production and exports, as there is no country within or outside the region that has the political incentive or military capabilities to establish physical control over the region's oil. Moreover, Azerbaijan and Kazakhstan, the two major oil producers, hope to produce as much oil as quickly as possible to maximize their revenues.

---

[9]Robert E. Ebel, "The National Security Implications of Oil," speech delivered to the Wilmington Club, Wilmington, DE, May 25, 1999. Ebel is the director of the Energy and National Security Program at the Center for Strategic and International Studies in Washington, D.C. There is a burgeoning literature on energy development in the Caspian region. Many of the recent publications show a more realistic appreciation of the region's energy potential than estimates that appeared in the 1990s, many of which, like official U.S. government projections, spawned wildly exaggerated expectations of the Caspian's promise. For balanced treatments of Caspian energy development, see Amy Myers Jaffe, "Unlocking the Assets: Energy Security and the Future of Central Asia and the Caucasus," paper prepared for the James A. Baker III Institute for Public Policy, Rice University, April 1998; Rosemarie Forsythe, *The Politics of Oil in the Caucasus and Central Asia*, Adelphi Paper 300, Oxford: Oxford University Press, 1996; John Roberts, *Caspian Pipelines*, London: Royal Institute of International Affairs, 1996; Robert E. Ebel, *Energy Choices in the Near Abroad: The Haves and the Have-Nots Face the Future*, Washington, D.C.: Center for Strategic and International Studies, April 1997; Laurent Ruseckas, "Energy and Politics in Central Asia and the Caucasus," *National Bureau of Asian Research Analysis*, Vol. 1, No. 2, July 1998; and Rajan Menon, "Treacherous Terrain: The Political and Security Dimensions of Energy Development in the Caspian Sea Zone," *National Bureau of Asian Research Analysis*, Vol. 9, No. 1, February 1998.

Nonetheless, the Caspian, like the Persian Gulf, is a volatile region that is conflict-prone and vulnerable to instability. In addition to market and economic conditions, both Kazakhstan and Azerbaijan will face two serious challenges to their ability to bring their oil to the international market: first, conflict and instability along planned pipeline routes for delivery of their long-term oil, and second, internal tensions and instability that could disrupt oil production. In addition, both countries would be vulnerable to decisions by regional governments such as Russia, Turkey, and Iran to use control over pipeline routes to extract political and economic concessions. Such decisions could at least temporarily reduce the quantity of Caspian oil exports.

The Vulnerability of Caspian Pipelines

There is no easy way to export energy from the Caspian Basin. Azerbaijan and Kazakhstan are landlocked and must therefore rely on the cooperation of neighboring countries—and subnational groups—to transport their energy to market. All the major east-west and north-south pipelines under consideration pass through regions that are wracked by conflict and unrest. Any Azeri oil headed north toward Russia or west toward the Mediterranean, for example, would be vulnerable to secessionist struggles in Georgia, a resumption of hostilities between Armenia and Azerbaijan over Nagorno-Karabakh, continuing Kurdish unrest in southeastern Turkey, and armed conflict in the Russian provinces of Chechnya and Daghestan. Kazakh oil destined to link up with any of the major east-west pipelines under consideration would have to transit the same areas.

An interdiction of Caspian Sea oil supplies resulting from terrorist or subnational attacks on oil pipelines and associated infrastructure would pose a serious challenge to the West and to Caspian oil-producing states. Even with the development of modern technologies to improve pipeline security, such as remote sensing, pipeline distribution systems remain vulnerable to military and cyber attack. If the pipeline is above ground, portions of it can be easily blown up using a variety of low-tech methods; even if the pipeline is buried, it is vulnerable to military and cyber attack at its exposed and usually undefended pumping stations, input terminals, river crossings, and intersystem connections. For instance, any one of the many points on the trans-Arabian pipeline could, if damaged or destroyed, halt product movement. Destroying pumping stations may cripple the use of a pipeline for up to six months. The centralized, computerized control of pipeline systems that enables valves to be opened or closed and pumps to be started or stopped remotely is also vulnerable to attack. Natural gas pipelines are especially vulnerable to interdiction because they must maintain a constant flow of pressure.

Consequently, safeguarding pipeline distribution systems against sabotage in conflict-ridden regions poses an extremely difficult challenge. The isolated and rugged terrain surrounding Caspian pipelines is not hospitable to conventional military operations but is well suited to guerrilla and mountain warfare; Western ground forces would be vulnerable to hit-and-run attacks, harassment, and acts of terrorism. In addition, the region's infrastructure to support pipeline defense operations is primitive, and Western military forces would be operating at the long end of a vulnerable logistics supply line. The use of combat aircraft or other airborne surveillance assets to patrol pipeline routes is not well suited to counter unconventional or guerrilla attacks. To be effective, therefore, the defense of pipelines would require a considerable commitment of forces that, at the very least, would exacerbate an already-serious operational tempo and readiness problem. Put simply, the use of force to ensure the protection of Caspian pipelines would not be an appropriate or effective response to a threat that, under the worst-case scenario, would affect only 2 percent of the world's oil supply for the next several years. More important, Western military intervention in a Caspian conflict is unlikely given the risk of a Russian military response.

The Vulnerability of Caspian States

A second potential threat to the flow of Caspian oil arises from internal tensions and upheaval in Kazakhstan and/or Azerbaijan. Over the next ten to fifteen years, these countries could confront a variety of challenges to internal stability, including tribal, ethnic, and clan disputes; severe poverty and growing disparities in income distribution; political repression and the absence of constitutional mechanisms for the orderly transfer of power; rapid population growth; mass urbanization; conflict over natural resources (e.g., oil, water, and land); and pervasive corruption, crime, and cronyism. In short, Kazakhstan and Azerbaijan display all the problems that can result in "failed states." Internal cleavages in both countries could trigger upheaval that would interfere with oil production in several ways, including discouraging foreign investment in oil operations and driving foreign oil workers to flee the country. Even more worrisome, internal conflict could feature attempts by rival factions to gain control of oil production facilities, which might result in damage to these installations.

Turmoil in Kazakhstan. Over the next decade, there is a potential for conflict between the ethnic Kazakh and Russian populations of Kazakhstan. Tensions between these two groups have increased over the past several years, fueled by rising nationalist sentiment on both sides. Kazakhstan's President Nursultan Nazarbayev has so far managed to keep a lid on virulent nationalism on both sides. Nonetheless, the presence of a large and increasingly disenchanted Russian minority in Kazakhstan's northern region adjacent to Russia presents a potentially volatile problem. Nazarbayev's eventual departure, the absence of a viable succession mechanism, and the rise of Kazakh nationalism portend a substantial risk of serious tensions with ethnic Russians, which could trigger civil war, the possible secession of Kazakhstan's northern provinces, or even Russian occupation of part or all of the country.

In addition, there is a potential for internecine strife among different Kazakh groups. The concentration of power in the hands of Nazarbayev and his clan has led to political stability in the short run; however, it threatens long-term stability by inflaming tribal, political, and economic grievances. Among those most alienated are the majority of the urban population and minority groups in resource-rich western Kazakhstan.

Upheaval in Azerbaijan. In the early years of independence, the regime in Azerbaijan was highly unstable, experiencing three leadership changes and numerous coup attempts. Since 1993, President Heydar Aliyev has brought stability to the country, but the longer-term political outlook is uncertain. Azerbaijan is ridden by internal cleavages among various ethnic groups and tribes. In particular, there is a simmering dispute between ethnic Azeris and the Persian population of Azerbaijan that would take only a small spark to ignite.

Such a conflict could spill over into northern Iran, which is inhabited by 20 million Azeris—twice as many as live in Azerbaijan. A full-scale civil war in Azerbaijan, with one faction supported by Tehran, could also provoke Iranian military intervention. Hence, internal conflict could not only disrupt oil production but also threaten a conflict between Azerbaijan and Iran that could lead to the military involvement of Turkey, Armenia, and Russia.

NORTH AFRICA

North Africa is likely to loom larger in the European energy picture in the years ahead and could shape broader perceptions of security requirements. The Maghreb is a leading exporter of natural gas to Western Europe, and Spain, Italy, and France are dependent on these supplies to meet a large portion of their energy requirements. Their substantial and growing imports of North African gas has spurred substantial investments in the expansion of production and transport infrastructure, including new regional and trans-Mediterranean pipelines (most notably the trans-Maghreb line from Algeria to Spain via Morocco and the expansion of the trans-Mediterranean line to Italy via Tunisia). As a result, energy trade is becoming a more central part of the security environment as seen from both sides of the Mediterranean. Indeed, the perception that a prolonged cutoff of North African natural gas supplies would have serious implications for the security of southern members of the Alliance has sparked heightened interest among these countries in making plans and preparations to respond to potential energy emergencies to the south. A central element in the energy nexus between Southern Europe and North Africa is the relative inflexibility of gas supply relationships. Unlike oil, gas is a regional rather than a global commodity. Expensive delivery infrastructure, once in place, creates a pattern of dependence among producers, transshipment states, and consumers that is structural.[10] Therefore, it is not surprising that NATO's southern allies are increasingly concerned about energy security. Evidence of this can be seen in the extent to which gas-

---

[10]For Western Europe as a whole, energy imports from North Africa represent less than 20 percent of total consumption. For Southern Europe, however, the dependence is far higher, with Portugal 90 percent, Spain 70 percent, and Italy 50 percent dependent on Algeria for gas needs alone.

related issues now dominate European perceptions of internal developments in Algeria.

Scenarios threatening the security of access to North African oil and gas could arise from internal, regional, or extraregional developments.

Internal Risks

It is most unlikely that regime change in North Africa—even the advent of radical anti-Western leaderships (as once feared in Algeria)—would lead to cutoffs of supply given the extraordinary importance of energy exports to the Algerian and Libyan economies. In Algeria, high levels of violence have thus far had only a marginal effect on energy operations, and it has not stopped investment in new energy projects. The remoteness of the oil and gas fields provides a buffer against terrorist attack, and the Algerian government devotes considerable resources to maintaining the security of energy-related infrastructure. Nonetheless, chaos and anarchy could threaten production or give rise to short-term strategies of disruption, including terrorist attacks on production facilities and pipelines. Under other circumstances, energy infrastructure could be a target of more organized and systematic attacks.

Regional Risks

A second class of scenarios flows from regional conflicts in which energy could be a direct or indirect target. Morocco and Algeria have a history of competition, outright conflict (e.g., the "War of the Sandsi" in the 1960s), and proxy war in the Western Sahara. The advent of a radical Islamist or, more likely, a nationalist regime in Algiers, or the renewal of Algerian intervention in the Western Sahara, could spark a new conflict that threatens the security of the trans-Maghreb pipeline. In the absence of radical agendas in Algiers or Rabat, however, the existence of the pipeline link may serve to dampen rather than inflame this bilateral competition, as both Moroccan and Algerian revenues would be at stake.

This scenario is mirrored to some extent in the eastern Maghreb in relations between Libya and Tunisia. There have been cross-border incidents in the past, and the Libyan threat is a continuing concern of Tunisian defense planners. Like Morocco, Tunisia is an important transit state for Algerian and Libyan energy exports.

There is continuing potential for conflict over the control of the Spanish enclaves of Ceuta and Melilla on the Moroccan coast opposite Gibraltar. The post-Hassan regime in Morocco could use the enclaves as a nationalist rallying point, and Madrid is committed to their defense (they are outside the NATO area but within the Western European Union [WEU] sphere of responsibility). Any military confrontation over the enclaves poses a risk of escalation, and gas flow across the Strait of Gibraltar could thus be disrupted. More seriously, the very large tanker traffic through the region could be affected by military operations or mining. This could have global implications for energy markets.[11]

Extraregional Risks

During the Gulf War, there was considerable concern in Europe that public sympathy for Baghdad across North Africa, coupled with the unpredictability of the Libyan leadership, could produce a north-south confrontation in the Mediterranean. Future instances of Western (including Israeli) intervention in the Gulf or elsewhere in the Middle East could raise similar risks. Against a backdrop of regime changes or the use of southern European bases for Western power projection, such risks could become tangible, with energy exports as the principal stake. Thus, the energy security outlook in North Africa is linked in important ways to developments in other regions, especially the Gulf.

Finally, North Africa contains one leading proliferator, Libya, and a potential proliferator, Algeria.[12] This increases the potential for confrontations over WMD production (e.g., the Libyan chemical facilities) that could spill over to affect energy security. As in the Gulf,

---

[11]For a discussion of the geopolitics of Mediterranean gas trade, see George Joffe, "The Euro-Mediterranean Partnership: Two Years After Barcelona," *Middle East Briefing*, No. 44, May 1998, p. 2.

[12]See Ian Lesser and Ashley Tellis, *Strategic Exposure: Proliferation Around the Mediterranean*, RAND, MR-742-A, 1996.

it also complicates any U.S. or European intervention to secure access to the region's energy resources.

Obviously, these internal, regional, and extraregional scenarios are not mutually exclusive; rather, they are parallel and potentially reinforcing. Unlike the Gulf and the Caspian, where vulnerable producers are distant from the Euro-Atlantic area, North Africa is on NATO's doorstep. Europe's relatively strong energy stake and the Maghreb's proximity to southern Europe make this an area where NATO's southern members could be motivated to request NATO assistance in an energy-related crisis, for example, to provide military assistance to protect key installations in response to a request from a local government. Proximity and the likelihood of smaller-scale contingencies also suggest that European forces could play the primary role, with support from key U.S. command, control, and communications (C^3), transport, and surveillance assets.

CONCLUSION

Over the next ten to fifteen years, a variety of threats could interfere with Western access to energy supplies from the Persian Gulf, the Caspian Basin, and North Africa. They include:

- military aggression in which critical oil production and transportation facilities are seized by Iraq or Iran;

- civil wars, coups, internal upheaval, and terrorism that would shut down the flow of energy from major energy-producing regions for a prolonged period;

- regional and domestic conflicts that would reduce but not halt energy supplies; and

- decisions by national governments that could curtail oil production and exports, thus affecting geopolitical alignments in critical regions.

These distinctions are important because they would affect perceptions of energy security and hence decisions by allied governments to use force to ensure access to energy supplies. The first threat, invasion with a view toward controlling key oil-producing installations, remains a key focus of U.S. defense planning. The consequences of these facilities' falling under the control of a government hostile to Western interests merit continued vigilance on the part of the West to ensure that such an invasion continues to be deterred or, if it happens, that the invasion could be halted before achieving its goal.

Second, would-be regional hegemons might take actions that threaten the external security of key energy-producing states, but not necessarily the unrestricted flow of oil.

Third, threats to the security of moderate, pro-Western Gulf Arab oil producers could fall well short of outright aggression or larger-scale conventional military operations. These threats could include the "coercive" use of force ranging from threatening force deployments and the demonstrative use of force to terrorism, sabotage, subversion, unconventional military operations, and limited seizure of territory or assets.

Fourth, many of these contingencies do not lend themselves as readily to a classical military response as cross-border invasion. Nonetheless, they are quite plausible and could have serious consequences for American interests and Western security. This is particularly true for internal instability or civil war in Saudi Arabia— the one scenario, given likely conditions in the world oil market over the next decade, that could have a profoundly negative effect on the global economy.

The foregoing discussion points to several implications. For at least the next five years and probably longer, the primary threat posed by both Iran and Iraq to Western interests in the Gulf are WMD, terrorism, and limited military operations, rather than large-scale invasion of a Gulf state. Clearly, the effects of a successful invasion could be so far-reaching that it cannot be ignored, and plans should continue to focus on deterring an invasion. But the United States should also seek allied military contributions across the full spectrum of contingencies that could disrupt oil flows. In many of these scenarios, allies may have specialized capabilities that could be effective in dealing with the conflict at hand, especially if U.S. forces are preoccupied with major military commitments elsewhere.

In weighing their own decisions to commit forces to secure energy supplies, most allies will consider whether the stakes are physical access to oil or other U.S. geopolitical interests that they may not necessarily share. For instance, even though the United States might feel compelled to use military force in the Persian Gulf to prevent the rise of a regional hegemon or to punish terrorist acts or NBC use, the European allies may be less inclined to join the United States in these military operations if secure access to oil is not at stake.

Many potential future threats to the flow of Persian Gulf and North African energy are internal, stemming from deep-seated political, economic, and social grievances. Because many challenges to the security of existing regimes may emanate from subnational actors, these threats, while important, fall outside of the set of challenges that can be addressed by external military action. The same is true, of course, for political decisions to increase oil prices by reducing oil production.

Chapter Three

THE ALLIES AND ENERGY SECURITY: PERSPECTIVES AND POLICIES

Richard Sokolsky, F. Stephen Larrabee, and Ian Lesser

There is growing interest within NATO—reflected in the Strategic Concept and in the DCI—in developing power projection capabilities for a wider range of missions than was the case during the Cold War. Moreover, the poor performance of European forces in Kosovo has galvanized European allies to improve their capability to project force outside NATO territory. Some allies, notably the U.K. and France, have made improvements in this area. It is by no means certain, however, that improved power projection capabilities will lead to a greater European willingness to use military force outside Europe in concert with the United States. Indeed, in contrast to the Cold War mission of collective defense, the allied use of force beyond Europe will be a matter of choice rather than obligation.

This chapter examines the attitudes and policies of America's European allies toward the use of force to protect Western energy security. It focuses in particular on the question of which allies the United States could count on, and under what conditions, to conduct military operations outside Europe to protect energy supplies. The initial section looks at the issue of energy security in a broader transatlantic context. The second section presents a historical overview of the Alliance's efforts to adapt its organization and forces for military operations beyond Europe. The third section surveys allied attitudes toward energy security and coalition operations, while the fourth section examines political constraints on coalition operations. The fifth section offers some observations about the future of coalition operations in key energy-producing regions, taking into account the factors that are likely to condition allied decisions to use force outside Europe. The final section draws some implications for U.S. military planning.

ENERGY SECURITY IN THE TRANSATLANTIC CONTEXT

Since the collapse of the Berlin Wall, NATO has made significant progress in addressing new threats and challenges in the post–Cold War security environment. During the Cold War, NATO's primary purpose was the defense of Alliance territory against a possible Soviet military attack. Over the past decade, this narrow strategic orientation has given way to a broader interest in projecting security and stability in and around Europe. The Alliance's new Strategic Concept, approved at the April 1999 NATO Summit in Washington, is emblematic of this new commitment. In the new concept, Alliance leaders declared that NATO's new role is to extend stability and security throughout the Euro-Atlantic region. They also agreed that non–Article 5 missions (e.g., those not involving direct defense of Alliance territory, such as peacekeeping and humanitarian operations) are now a core NATO mission. Finally, to give substance to these new commitments, NATO leaders approved the DCI, which is designed to improve Alliance members' ability to project force effectively across the full spectrum of its missions.

Nonetheless, NATO's transformation remains incomplete. The Strategic Concept does not directly address one of the principal challenges facing the Western allies in the next millennium: threats to common security interests emanating from beyond Europe. Indeed, although the Strategic Concept has given direction to NATO's post–Cold War mission in Europe, it has failed to resolve the question of NATO's role outside Europe, especially in preserving security in regions of vital interest to the West, such as the Persian Gulf. The continuing differences within the Alliance surrounding the circumstances under which NATO would use force outside Europe could create strains in transatlantic relations over the next decade.

Although NATO's energies in the coming years will be consumed by peacekeeping and peace support missions in Europe and by the implementation of a long-term stabilization plan for the Balkans, ensuring Western access to energy supplies is likely to emerge as an increasingly divisive issue for the United States and its European allies. For the past half century, Europe has imported large quantities of oil from the Persian Gulf and has been a prime beneficiary of the American security umbrella in the region. Paradoxically, however, the United States—which is considerably less dependent on Persian Gulf oil than Europe—has assumed the role of guarantor of Persian Gulf security at considerable expense in national resources and political capital.

In fact, with few exceptions, America's European allies lack the political will and the power projection capabilities to contribute meaningfully to the defense of the Persian Gulf against regional threats. Whether the United States will be willing to continue to bear a disproportionate share of this burden is questionable. There is mounting concern among senior U.S. military officials and members of Congress about the strains placed on U.S. forces by America's expanding worldwide military commitments. These expanding commitments are being borne by a force structure that is 35 percent smaller than a decade ago.[1] The added strains on U.S. military readiness from operations in Kosovo have exacerbated this concern.

Rising frustration over unequal sharing of security responsibilities within NATO, as well as the changing nature of the security threats the Alliance will face in the future, led the United States to press its European allies to increase their power projection capabilities. U.S. military commanders have also expressed concern about the growing gap between U.S. and European forces in high-tech military capabilities, which could make it difficult in the future for European countries to fight effectively in a coalition with U.S. forces.[2] Whether

---

[1]See Stephen Lee Myers, "Peace Strains the Army," *New York Times*, July 11, 1999. Concern over the impact of U.S. military commitments overseas on readiness has also led to a reported U.S. government decision to end the permanent presence of U.S. troops in Haiti. The Department of Defense, according to press reports, is also urging a drawdown of other U.S. forces engaged in peacekeeping and stability support operations. See Stephen Lee Myers, "G.I.'s to Quit Haiti; Reason Cited Is Budgetary," *New York Times*, August 26, 1999, and Elaine M. Grossman, "CENTCOM Chief Rejects New Call to Cut Forces Patrolling Iraqi Skies," *Inside the Pentagon*, August 26, 1999.

[2]For a cogent discussion of the growing transatlantic gap in military capabilities and technology, see David C. Gompert, Richard L. Kugler, and Martin C. Libicki, *Mind the Gap: Promoting a Transatlantic Revolution in Military Affairs*, Washington, D.C.: NDU Press, 1999.

America's European allies will heed the call for improving their power projection and coalition warfare capabilities remains uncertain. Most European governments have a strong aversion to NATO's use of force outside Europe, especially in the absence of a U.N. mandate, and allied governments face stiff domestic opposition to extending NATO's security responsibilities beyond the European continent.

The fault line between the U.S. and European perspectives on NATO's agenda and priorities outside Europe could remain dormant for some time as long as there is no major crisis in the Persian Gulf. However, prospects for long-term stability in the Gulf remain uncertain in light of the political, economic, and social strains that afflict traditional societies struggling to cope with the challenges of modernization. Furthermore, both Iraq and Iran are likely to jockey for influence in the region over the next decade, and their rivalry could lead to heightened tension and perhaps conflict. A serious Iraqi or Iranian military challenge to the security of the Arabian Peninsula and access to oil supplies could fracture Alliance unity if Western military intervention were required and if few of America's allies were able to make a meaningful contribution.

ADAPTING NATO FOR MILITARY OPERATIONS BEYOND EUROPE

The question of improving allied military capabilities to protect critical energy supplies is best understood within the broader context of the historical debate within the Alliance over the sensitive "out-of-area" issue and the new Strategic Concept's definition of NATO's future purpose. The United States has had a long-standing interest in securing a greater allied military contribution to the defense of the Persian Gulf. Indeed, U.S. initiatives to promote European cooperation in planning for and conducting joint military operations outside Europe have sparked intense controversy within NATO for more than 20 years.

The Historical Context

The cataclysmic events of 1979 thrust the out-of-area issue into the forefront of NATO's formal agenda. Following the twin shocks of the

Iranian Revolution and the Soviet invasion of Afghanistan, the United States pressed its NATO allies to assume more of the burden of improving the Western defense posture in Southwest Asia (SWA).[3] In a major campaign to shift the focus of NATO planning to the Persian Gulf, the United States urged allied governments to (1) increase force levels within Europe to compensate for the diversion of American forces to the defense of SWA; (2) make civilian and military aircraft and ships available to transport U.S. forces from the United States and Europe to the Persian Gulf in an emergency; (3) augment their peacetime military presence in the Persian Gulf and Indian Ocean; and (4) provide the necessary access, overflight, logistical, and transportation arrangements to support the deployment of U.S. forces in a crisis.

The European allies reacted coolly to American overtures. As a result, the Alliance made limited progress in developing capabilities for out-of-area operations. The U.K. and France made minimal improvements in their rapid-deployment capabilities and slightly increased their naval presence in the Arabian Sea. The United States concluded en route access and logistical support agreements with several European countries, including Portugal, Spain, and Germany, and secured U.K. cooperation in establishing a base on the Indian Ocean island of Diego Garcia. Some allies, notably Italy and Germany, agreed to "fill in behind" for U.S. naval forces that were redeployed to SWA by increasing their naval deployments in the Mediterranean and the north Atlantic, respectively. By the early 1980s, several European allies had earmarked hundreds of ships and aircraft to move U.S. forces in a Persian Gulf contingency.

At the same time, European countries balked at undertaking a formal NATO role in SWA and frequently failed to implement military measures that had been agreed to by Alliance political authorities. European countries, for example, rejected any kind of formal association with the United States' newly created Rapid Deployment Force and rebuffed American proposals for the creation of a NATO rapid action force. Similarly, allied governments resisted formalizing or coordinating multinational planning for out-of-area operations.

---

[3]For an excellent historical overview of Western security policy toward the Persian Gulf, see Charles A. Kupchan, *The Persian Gulf and the West*, Boston, MA: Allen and Unwin, 1987.

Consequently, the 1980s saw few major improvements in allied expeditionary capabilities or in NATO's machinery for planning and conducting joint military operations beyond Europe.[4]

The failure of the Alliance and individual member countries to adapt forces, plans, and procedures to the demands of military operations in a high-threat environment outside Europe was made abundantly clear by the meager allied contribution to Operation Desert Storm. NATO's formal response was limited primarily to defense of NATO's southern region. Twelve NATO countries contributed forces to the anti-Iraq coalition, and a handful supported air operations against Iraq mounted from Turkey (Spain, the U.K., France, Italy, and Greece). But only the U.K. and France contributed meaningful combat forces, and only with the United States providing the great bulk of strategic lift and initial logistics support for these deployments. The United States provided 75 percent of the combat aircraft, flew 85 percent of the combat sorties, and contributed roughly 90 percent of the ground forces that engaged in the ground offensive.[5]

Events in the early 1990s ushered in a new phase in NATO's out-of-area strategy. The end of the Cold War and the collapse of the Soviet Union and the Warsaw Pact removed two chief impediments to an enlarged Alliance role outside Europe: the fear of weakening defenses in Europe and anxiety over being dragged into unnecessary conflicts by the U.S.-Soviet rivalry. In equal measure, the Iraqi invasion of Kuwait and endemic instability in the Balkans poignantly illustrated how events on NATO's periphery and beyond Europe could threaten Western security interests.

Together, these developments—combined with the growing perception in the United States that European countries were not pulling their weight—galvanized the Alliance into adapting its strategy, missions, forces, and command structures to the dramatically transformed European security environment.[6] The Alliance's November

---

[4]Ibid.

[5]For a detailed account of NATO's role in Operation Desert Storm, see Jonathan T. Howe, "NATO and the Gulf Crisis," *Survival*, Vol. 33, No. 3, May-June 1991, pp. 246–259.

[6]"NATO's New Force Structures," NATO Basic Fact Sheet No. 5, Brussels, January 1996.

1991 Strategic Concept called on NATO members to develop the capabilities to deal with a broader range of missions and threats—including the capability to perform crisis management and peacekeeping operations. At the 1994 NATO Summit in Brussels, Alliance leaders approved several changes to NATO's political and military structures and procedures to enable the Alliance to conduct these diverse missions more effectively and efficiently. They also gave impetus to the growing European desire to bolster the European pillar of the Alliance by endorsing the concept of Combined Joint Task Forces (CJTF). When fully implemented, the CJTF will allow a coalition of like-minded NATO countries to use NATO assets and command structures to conduct non–Article 5 operations without the participation of U.S. forces and assets and without the consensus of all Alliance members.[7]

Throughout the 1990s, NATO continued to improve the way its forces were organized and maintained to react more rapidly to crises in and around Europe. In particular, NATO created more flexible and mobile forces, including the Allied Rapid Reaction Corps (ARRC), and improved coordination, joint planning, and command structures for missions on NATO's borders and beyond.[8] Indeed, the ARRC is envisioned as the Alliance's main vehicle for carrying out crisis management, peacekeeping, and related stability support operations. These new structures place greater emphasis on flexibility, mobility, and lethality. Furthermore, the reorganization of forces within NATO's Integrated Military Command structure reflects these force characteristics as well as the growing importance of multinational forces for coalition operations.

In parallel with the Alliance's formation of more flexible, mobile, and deployable force structures, several allied countries created their own rapid reaction forces and began to develop plans to employ these forces in multinational formations. Foremost among these are the German Crisis Reaction Forces (KRK), the United Kingdom's Joint Rapid Reaction Force, and the French Rapid Action Force

---

[7]For an in-depth discussion of the origins and implications of NATO's Combined Joint Task Forces, see Charles Barry, "NATO's Combined Joint Task Forces in Theory and Practice," *Survival*, Vol. 36, No. 3, Spring 1996, pp. 81–97.

[8]See Gregory Piatt, "NATO Adapts to Post–Cold War World," *European Stars and Stripes*, September 13, 1999.

(FAR). In addition, the Eurocorps, consisting of units from Belgium, France, Germany, Luxembourg, and Spain, has undertaken a limited amount of joint training and operational planning for multinational operations and has shared responsibility for command of the Kosovo Peacekeeping Force (KFOR) with other NATO commands. Finally, the WEU's formation of the European Force (EUROFOR) and the European Maritime Force (EUROMARFOR) is a potentially significant development of the EU's defense capabilities, especially since these forces are clearly designed for North African contingencies, including the preservation of access to energy supplies.

Although the shift in focus away from the Cold War mission of static defense of territorial borders is an important and long-overdue development, its significance for Alliance military operations outside Europe should not be exaggerated. The force enhancements mandated by the 1991 Strategic Concept were designed primarily to improve the capability of allied forces to deal with low-intensity missions and threats on the periphery of NATO territory.[9] Consequently, Alliance force planning has continued to attach a lower priority to improving NATO's power projection capability for the more distant and demanding military contingencies in the Gulf. For most of the past decade, therefore, only the U.K. and France (and to a much lesser extent the Netherlands) have made tangible improvements in their long-range power projection capability—and even they continue to have serious shortfalls in the critical areas of precision-guided munitions (PGMs), strategic lift, mobile logistics, and deployable command, control, communications, computing, intelligence, surveillance, and reconnaissance (C^4ISR).

The Way Ahead

The Strategic Concept approved at the April 1999 NATO Summit in Washington defines NATO's central purpose as establishing stability and security in the Euro-Atlantic area. Thus, a key unresolved issue confronting the Alliance is the functional and geographic scope of future NATO military operations outside this area: For what

---

[9]John E. Peters and Howard Deshong, *Out of Area or Out of Reach? European Military Support for Operations in Southwest Asia*, RAND, MR-629-OSD, 1995, p. 98.

purposes and where will the Alliance choose to use military force beyond Europe?

The Alliance's new Strategic Concept opened the door to, but stopped short of, establishing the political, doctrinal, and military underpinnings for concerted NATO action beyond Europe's borders. It recognizes non–Article 5 contingencies as a fundamental security task of the Alliance and acknowledges that extending stability and security throughout the Euro-Atlantic area can be put at risk by crises and conflicts affecting the security of the Euro-Atlantic area. It also acknowledges that Alliance security interests can be affected by other risks of a wider nature, including disruption of the flow of vital resources. Finally, the Alliance's new mission statement urges members to continue adapting NATO's forces, structures, and procedures to meet the full range of the Alliance's new missions.

That said, the Strategic Concept, while not foreclosing the option of Alliance power projection operations beyond Europe, does not identify securing access to vital oil supplies as a core NATO mission; similarly, it does not explicitly state that threats to the security of the Persian Gulf could affect the security of the Euro-Atlantic area, although it does indirectly imply it. As a consequence, there is no explicit mandate in the Strategic Concept to prepare Alliance power projection capabilities for major combat operations or for an MTW in the Persian Gulf or in other potentially important energy-producing regions. Equally important, the Strategic Concept is of limited utility in providing specific operational guidance to Alliance force planners. In fact, shorn of its rhetoric, the Strategic Concept is a blueprint for developing the capabilities to meet threats to peace and stability within Europe. It has very little to say concretely about meeting threats to Alliance security interests emanating from beyond Europe, although it does call attention to the growing threat posed by WMD.[10]

---

[10]Of course, improved coalition capabilities for crisis management and "peace support" operations on the fringes of Europe may produce some ancillary benefit, particularly improving the interoperability of coalition forces. However, achieving a higher degree of interoperability and standardization to meet the operational requirements of these specific missions should not be confused with meeting the operational requirements for large and complex combat operations or an MTW in the greater Middle East.

This outcome is hardly surprising given the constellation of political forces surrounding the Summit. The Strategic Concept was a compromise document that papered over fundamental differences between U.S. and European strategic priorities and perspectives in the post–Cold War environment. The United States is increasingly concerned with threats to common Western interests emanating from beyond Europe, especially the proliferation of NBC weapons and their means of delivery as well as threats to energy supplies in the Persian Gulf. Accordingly, the United States believes that the central purpose of the Alliance should be to defend common Western security interests both within Europe and beyond its borders.[11]

Reflecting this security agenda, the United States has prodded its NATO allies to shift the emphasis in NATO force planning from the defense of territory to projecting stability and security "in and beyond" Europe. From the U.S. perspective, meeting this challenge would require improving allied capabilities to (1) project significant force rapidly at great distances from NATO territory; (2) sustain these forces in high-intensity combat operations with limited access to NATO infrastructure; (3) conduct military operations in the presence of NBC weapons; and (4) operate effectively together as a multinational coalition. There is growing American interest, moreover, in allied development of both theater and national missile defense capabilities to defend allied territory against long-range ballistic missile attack by states that might in the future commit aggression against countries friendly to the West outside Europe. Without these capabilities, in the view of its proponents, states contemplating such aggression may calculate that European countries could be deterred from coming to the assistance of threatened states owing to the vulnerability of their territory to ballistic missile attack. If this were to occur, Europe could risk becoming decoupled from the United States if this vulnerability coerced them into rejecting participation in coalition operations to defend common Western interests.

---

[11]For a clear exposition of this perspective by senior American officials, see Strobe Talbott, "The New Europe and the New NATO," speech delivered to the German Society for Foreign Policy, Bonn, Germany, February 4, 1999; Thomas R. Pickering, "The Transatlantic Partnership: A History of Defending Freedom; A Future for Extending It," speech delivered to the SACLANT Conference, Norfolk, VA, October 30, 1998; and Marc Grossman, "The Future of the U.S.-Europe Relationship," speech delivered to the Houston World Affairs Council, October 1, 1998.

At the same time, however, many Europeans have rejected this expansive and ambitious conception of the Alliance's future role.[12] Most European governments are concerned primarily with threats to security within Europe or on its immediate periphery, and their forces (with the exception of the U.K. and France and increasingly Germany and Italy) thus remain focused largely on the defense of borders rather than on power projection capabilities. Furthermore, most allies believe that NATO's main mission should lie in preserving security, supporting stability, and managing crises "in and around" Europe. For most European governments, parliaments, and publics, this means the Balkans and the Mediterranean but certainly not the Gulf or the Transcaucasus.

Therefore, in contrast to growing U.S. appeals to extend NATO's missions and capabilities beyond Europe, most European governments are quite content with having the means to engage only in low-intensity "stability support operations," which fall well short of what would be needed to defeat a well-armed adversary—especially one that possessed NBC weapons—in high-intensity combat operations. The narrow European vision of NATO's purposes is reflected in the missions of the emerging European Security and Defense Policy (ESDP), whose primary focus is low-level crisis management, peacekeeping, and peace support operations—the so-called "Petersberg tasks." In addition, the lack of European interest in developing the capabilities to meet threats to Alliance security emanating from outside Europe is reflected in the tepid allied interest in ballistic missile defenses and continued allied foot dragging in implementing the Alliance's 1994 counterproliferation program. Simply put, most allies are reluctant to spend scarce resources to deal with what they perceive as a remote threat, especially since such expenditures would almost certainly come at the expense of acquiring the capabilities to deal with threats in Europe's backyard under the banner of the ESDP.

At the NATO Summit in Washington, the gap between U.S. and European perspectives on the out-of-area issue was bridged through

---

[12]Joseph Fitchett, "A More United Europe Worries About Globalizing NATO," *International Herald Tribune*, December 31, 1998; David Buchan, "U.S. Urges NATO to Take On Wider Role," *Financial Times*, December 7, 1998; and Roger Cohen, "A Policy Struggle Stirs Within NATO," *New York Times*, November 28, 1998.

mutual compromises and accommodation: The United States was forced to scale back its expectations with respect to the declaration of the Alliance's new purposes. From a theological standpoint, therefore, the European allies gained American acquiescence to a Strategic Concept that avoids expressing an explicit Alliance commitment to extend its security umbrella beyond Europe. But the European allies had to accept a broader definition of threats to "common interests." Moreover, they approved a DCI that could lead to significant improvements in allied power projection capabilities for missions lying beyond the defense of allied territory.

The main purpose of the DCI is to improve Alliance defense capabilities to ensure effective multinational operations across the full spectrum of Alliance missions in the new security environment.[13] The DCI responds to four key challenges:

- First, the need to adapt NATO forces so that the Alliance can address the security problems and demands generated by the new strategic environment. The most likely challenges NATO will face in the future are ethnic strife, regional conflicts, the proliferation of NBC weapons, and threats to energy supplies. Most of these threats will arise on Europe's borders and beyond and will change the character of future NATO military operations. In particular, many future non–Article 5 power projection missions will be smaller in scale than the Cold War mission of territorial defense. They may also be longer in duration, involve multinational operations below division level, and be undertaken without full access to existing NATO infrastructure. To meet these threats and challenges, NATO countries must develop more mobile, flexible, sustainable, and survivable forces to conduct coalition operations beyond allied territory.

- Second, the need to incorporate critical technologies, especially in the area of command-and-control and information systems, and to address the accelerating pace of technological change and the different rate at which allies are introducing these advanced capabilities into their force structures. A major purpose of the

---

[13]"NATO Summit Press Release on the DCI," Washington, D.C., April 25, 1999.

DCI is to narrow and eventually close the gap that has emerged between U.S. and European military-technological capabilities.

- Third, the need to agree on a common core of allied military capabilities, including the ability to share a much greater volume of battlefield data, coordinate operations, and conduct effective multinational operations across the full spectrum of possible military contingencies. Embedded in the DCI is the notion of a "common operational vision" that will lead to greater standardization of military doctrine, organization, tactics, training, and operational procedures to fully exploit the military-operational benefits of advanced technologies.

- Fourth, the need for all NATO countries to acquire the capability to protect their forces from NBC attacks and to operate on a battlefield contaminated by these weapons.

The DCI reflects these priorities and is aimed at fostering improved allied capabilities in five areas:

- **Deployability.** Despite some of the improvements several allies have made in their power projection capabilities, only the United States is capable of deploying large forces promptly outside NATO territory. To redress this deficiency, the DCI calls for NATO countries to (1) develop modular, self-sufficient force packages that can be readily tailored to the needs of specific missions; (2) better train personnel for power projection operations, especially small-unit operations, and move toward more professional armed forces; (3) procure equipment that is more easily transportable; and (4) improve capabilities for long-range military transport.

- **Sustainability.** Most of our NATO allies lack the structures, stockpiles, flexibility, and interoperability to sustain operations for both peacekeeping and power projection, particularly integrated multinational operations in a high-threat environment. There is a need, for example, to promote closer cooperation among the Alliance's combat service support and logistics units, especially logistic echelon above corps (EAC), and to achieve greater interoperability and standardization in logistics operations. EAC logistics support will be especially important in future military operations beyond NATO territory because of the special demands they place on the Alliance's logistical system, including deployment of port operations units, heavy construction engineer battalions, long-haul or heavy-lift transportation assets, and other combat service support needed for large-scale operations in remote theaters with limited military infrastructure. Unlike the U.S. force structure, most European militaries lack EAC logistics units as well as significant deployable logistic support elements. Similarly, many European allies maintain low stockpiles of critical logistics items, including munitions, fuel, food, and medical supplies.

- **Effective engagement.** Many European allies lack the modern equipment, firepower, and advanced technologies with which to engage an adversary across the full spectrum of conflict. A particularly acute problem is the growing gap between American and European forces in their exploitation of so-called Revolution in Military Affairs (RMA) technologies—a problem compounded by the slow pace of European force modernization. Together, these issues have created potentially significant interoperability problems and, more important, would make it extremely difficult for allied forces to conduct fully integrated ground, sea, and air operations. In addition, many allies are limited in the amount of firepower they can bring to bear owing to shortages in PGMs and information systems to exploit these capabilities by achieving full situational awareness of the battlefield.

- **Survivability of forces and infrastructure.** The vulnerability of individual allied countries and Alliance forces to NBC weapons poses a potentially serious impediment to effective coalition power projection operations. There are two key dimensions to this problem. First, the vulnerability of national infrastructure and populations to NBC (or terrorist) attack could discourage countries from participating in or supporting coalition operations. Second, most European allies lack the equipment and capabilities to protect their deployed forces against NBC attack and to operate effectively in a contaminated environment; in particular, most have fallen far behind the United States in achieving the Alliance's NBC-related force goals, such as protective equipment, wide-area ground surveillance, chemical and biological warfare (CBW) detection systems, and countermeasures against CBW agents. Moreover, many have failed to adapt their doctrines, force structures, operations, and logistics practices to meet the unique demands imposed by power projection operations in a NBC environment; for example, none of the allies has given its deployed forces "just in time" logistics and self-protection capabilities to avoid presenting lucrative, massed targets. Unless these deficiencies are corrected and the gap is closed between U.S. and European capabilities to project and protect forces in a WMD environment, the Alliance will face serious difficulties in achieving a high level of interoperability among units in multinational formations and in executing a successful military campaign. Moreover, if these problems are left to fester, NATO could see a dwindling number of allied forces available for non–Article 5 operations.

- **Command, control, and communications.** The differing capabilities of Alliance members to exchange information could hinder interoperability and the effectiveness of coalition operations. Indeed, power projection for non–Article 5 operations, unlike the national layer-cake, theater-scale operations that dominated NATO planning and force development for Cold War Article 5 missions, puts much greater stress on both tactical and strategic C^3. To ensure military effectiveness in future operations, which are likely to be multinational and quite often involve brigade-size units, NATO will need a joint and combined command-and-control capability. Most important, the Alliance must acquire the capability to collect, process, and disseminate an uninterrupted flow of critical information while exploiting or denying an enemy's ability to do the same thing. To attain these objectives, NATO will need to field interoperable C^3 systems and information assurance capabilities on a much broader scale based on a more common set of standards.[14]

European capabilities for projecting force in future military contingencies outside Europe must also be evaluated in the context of the EU's commitment to establishing a common ESDP. At the December 1999 summit in Helsinki, EU leaders announced the formation of a rapid reaction force of 50,000 to 60,000 troops capable of

---

[14]The authors are indebted to RAND colleagues John Peters and William O'Malley for their contribution to the discussion of the DCI.

being deployed anywhere in Europe in 60 days for up to one year. How will this force—and the evolving arrangements for NATO-EU cooperation in European crisis management—affect the commitment of America's European allies to improve their power projection capabilities under NATO's DCI?

The structure and capabilities of the ESDP, as well as its relationship with NATO and non-EU NATO allies, remain a work in progress. At this juncture, it is an open question whether EU members will be able to muster the political will and resources to achieve real military capabilities, given declining defense budgets, demands for increased social spending, the divergent foreign policy interests and perspectives of EU members, and an unwieldy EU bureaucracy that lacks the experience and culture for dealing with military and security issues. Indeed, many observers fear that the EU will miss its goal of fielding the rapid reaction corps by 2003 or, as one U.S. official has lamented, use "smoke and mirrors" and other accounting gimmicks to reach its "headline" goals.[15] Similarly, many U.S. officials worry that the ESDP could lead to a wasteful duplication of NATO assets, alienate NATO members who are not members of the EU, and create competing defense structures that will complicate a coordinated NATO and EU response to future crises.[16] If this were to occur, the EU's new structures and procedures would weaken NATO, and the ESDP would be a "Potemkin" force dependent on U.S. and NATO capabilities for all but the most minor tasks.

Although it is too soon to draw any definitive conclusions concerning the impact of the ESDP on allied power projection capabilities pending the resolution of these and other issues, several preliminary observations seem in order:

- First, the European rapid reaction force is being designed explicitly to handle the so-called Petersberg tasks of crisis man-

---

[15]James Kittfield, "European Doughboys," *National Journal*, February 26, 2000.

[16]William Drozdiak, "U.S. Tepid on European Defense Plan," *Washington Post*, March 7, 2000; William Pfaff, "Falling Out Over European Defense," *International Herald Tribune*, April 13, 2000; Joseph Fitchett, "EU Takes Steps to Create a Military Force Without Treading on NATO," *International Herald Tribune*, March 1, 2000; and Frederick Bonnart, "U.S. Starts to Fret Over EU Military Independence," *International Herald Tribune*, May 24, 2000.

agement, peacekeeping, and humanitarian operations within Europe. Although the Petersberg mandate embraces a full spectrum of operations, up to and including peacemaking operations of the kind the Alliance conducted against Serbia, its emphasis is on the low end of the spectrum (peacekeeping and humanitarian operations). To date the connection between the DCI and the ESDP remains fuzzy, leading some observers to worry that NATO could become a two-tier alliance in which European countries handle light peacekeeping duties in a benign environment while leaving serious military operations to the United States and NATO.

- Second, the European rapid reaction force will consist of lightly armed ground forces. Although it will probably have strategic transport and naval units assigned to it, it is unlikely to be structured to deploy significant air and ground forces over long distances. Nor is it likely to have the infrastructure and logistics base to sustain these forces in high-intensity combat operations for a prolonged period. Further, as long as some countries retain conscription, it will be difficult to deploy these forces in high-threat environments.

- Third, it cannot be taken for granted that the capabilities European allies might acquire to implement the ESDP will necessarily contribute to the DCI; in fact, there is potential for tension to arise between implementation of these two initiatives. As previously noted, the main purpose of the DCI is to improve the Alliance's ability to conduct effective multinational operations across the full spectrum of Alliance missions. To be sure, strengthening the ability of European allies to conduct low-end peacekeeping operations, either within an Alliance framework or outside it when NATO as a whole is not engaged, will contribute to that goal and thus lead to more equitable burden sharing within the Alliance. For example, the European strategic lift that would be used to transport EU peacekeeping units to a European trouble spot would also be available to ferry European ground forces to the Persian Gulf. Nonetheless, the focus of the DCI is clearly on improving allied power projection and allied capabilities to fight together effectively in coalition operations with the United States. In other words, except for a small set of modest contingencies, where assets for the DCI and the ESDP may overlap, the military capabilities needed to carry out their different missions appear to be largely incompatible.

- Fourth, the EU's pursuit of the ESDP, especially if strong institutional links are not established between the EU and NATO, could come at the expense of the DCI and the ability of Alliance members to contribute in a more meaningful way to coalition military operations outside Europe. This is likely to be the case for several reasons:

  — European defense budgets are declining, and resources for DCI programs, many of which are expensive, will now face competing claims from the ESDP. Many European governments will find it difficult to resist the temptation to utilize existing forces for the ESDP rather than create new capabilities. Moreover, it will be easier for many countries to mobilize public support for increased defense spending in support of an EU enterprise than for bolstering capabilities for military operations outside Europe that are unpopular.

  — Many of the forces and assets that will be required for the ESDP already have NATO commitments. If these forces are restructured for ESDP-related tasks, and especially if EU planning for these missions is not done in close cooperation with NATO's defense planning process, the ESDP could weaken rather than strengthen NATO. Indeed, unless full transparency and formalized institutional links are established between the EU and NATO, a situation could arise in which forces that are "dual hatted" could face conflicting guidance from EU and NATO defense planners.

None of this is meant to suggest that development of the ESDP is bad for NATO; to the contrary, if it is managed correctly and improved European capabilities are developed within NATO, the ESDP could strengthen NATO and transatlantic ties, since forces and capabilities that are developed for EU-led operations will be available to NATO as well. Likewise, the EU's failure to realize its ambitions for a common ESDP could fuel sentiments at home for U.S. disengagement from Europe. In short, a weak Europe that is incapable of shouldering its fair share of security responsibilities poses a far greater threat to healthy transatlantic relations than a strong Europe that, when NATO decides to opt out, can lead peacekeeping and crisis management operations in Europe, even if they are on a small scale. That said, the ESDP, if it becomes a reality, is a necessary but not sufficient condition for achieving a more equitable distribution of risks and burdens within the Alliance and for closing the gap in capabilities and missions between the United States and its European allies. If Europe and the United States are to establish a more mature and equal partnership, the DCI and related efforts to improve the power projection capabilities of European militaries must not be sacrificed at the altar of the ESDP.

Whatever the EU does regarding the ESDP, there should be one set of military forces between the EU and NATO, and the goals of both organizations should be compatible. In short, the EU military force that is created should be capable of performing more ambitious tasks than just low-intensity peacekeeping. The Europeans, moreover, will need to harmonize their force structures with NATO's implementation of the DCI to ensure consistency between NATO and EU developments.

In sum, the DCI provides a framework for improving allied power projection capabilities and the capability of the Alliance to conduct effective and integrated multinational operations. The extent to which the allies realize these improvements will depend on several issues: Do the allies have the political will and resources to implement the DCI at the same time the EU is moving ahead with the ESDP?[17] Even if they overcome many of the military constraints on

---

[17]To date, the allies have achieved mixed results in implementing the DCI that was approved in April 1999. According to a recent Department of Defense report on the implementation of the DCI, the Alliance has made progress in some but not all of the program's five areas. Plans to improve Alliance logistics and C^3 capabilities are well under way, but efforts to enhance capabilities in the other three functional categories are lagging behind. As one senior Pentagon official informed Congress, however, implementing the DCI requires increases in defense spending and a reallocation of resources across the Alliance—especially for force restructuring—that many allied governments have resisted. Of particular concern is Germany, which recently announced its plans to cut defense spending by $10 billion over the next four years and whose forces require significant restructuring. The prospect that these defense budget cuts will be rescinded is dim, and the German Ministry of Defense, which has championed increased spending and force restructuring, appears resigned to the fact that any DCI-related force enhancements will need to be made through reprogramming of existing defense spending allocations. See Catherine MacRae, "DOD Reports on Progress of NATO's Defense Capabilities Initiative," *Inside the Pentagon*, March 16, 2000.

coalition operations, is the Alliance likely to approve a NATO military operation in regional conflicts that threaten Western energy supplies?   How much consensus is there within the Alliance on this mission? To what extent do the allies see the Persian Gulf, the Caspian, and North Africa as regions for NATO military involvement? What are the key political constraints on coalition operations? Which allies can the U.S. rely on the most to conduct such operations? In what contingencies would these allies be prepared to use force to protect energy supplies, and under what command arrangements?

THE ALLIES AND MILITARY OPERATIONS OUTSIDE EUROPE

The history of the U.S.-European dispute over NATO military operations outside Europe, especially in preparing for high-intensity conflict, reveals several trends:

*   First, progress in developing allied military capabilities for such missions has been slow and uneven: After 20 years of U.S. cajoling, only a handful of NATO allies can bring significant combat forces to the table in U.S.-led coalition operations in a Persian Gulf MTW. Moreover, British and French motivations for participating in these operations are largely political, raising questions about how far and how fast both are prepared to go in improving their power projection capabilities. For the most part, they see developing the military capabilities for these missions as the entry price for protecting their equities in the region and, especially in the case of the U.K., maintaining transatlantic ties. By contrast, several European countries possess the capabilities to make a more serious contribution to military operations in North Africa.

*   Second, what progress has been made was due primarily to U.S. pressure and the resulting European fears that failure to meet U.S. expectations could erode the U.S. commitment to NATO and the transatlantic relationship. There is little evidence to suggest, in light of the Alliance's reaction to the Soviet invasion of Afghanistan, Iraq's invasion of Kuwait, and Saddam Hussein's blatant challenge to the U.N. sanctions regime in Iraq, that most

European countries have fundamentally changed their strategic orientation toward the Persian Gulf. Simply put, only U.S. leadership and pressure have brought about changes in the allied perspective on the out-of-area issue.

- Third, external events have had a much greater impact in shaping European attitudes toward the use of force beyond Europe than official communiqués articulating NATO's purposes. This suggests that the Alliance has been in a reactive, ad hoc mode and has not evolved a more forward-looking strategic outlook based on a larger geopolitical vision of the Alliance's future.

The past, of course, may not necessarily be a prologue to the future. At least in the short term, the Strategic Concept, implementation of the DCI, and the EU's development of real military capabilities will likely lead to improved allied capabilities for a broader range of non–Article 5 missions in and around Europe, particularly with continued prodding from senior U.S. government officials and pressure from Congress. How far and how fast the allies will move in this direction remain uncertain, however, except perhaps for the British and French. On the basis of current trends, the evidence is mixed if not contradictory. Clearly, several positive developments have occurred in the past few years in allied willingness and capability to participate in U.S.-led coalition operations:

- Several NATO countries have often contributed forces to U.S.-led multinational operations. The most frequent participants in these coalitions were the U.K., France, Turkey, Germany, Italy, and the Netherlands. On average, five NATO partners participated in U.S.-led multilateral operations that were not sanctioned by the U.N., and seven to eight NATO allies contributed to U.N.-authorized operations.

- Although defense spending in European countries is stagnant or falling, many allied governments, with the notable exception of Germany, have thus far resisted draconian defense budget cuts. In general, European governments have been able to satisfy popular demands for a "peace dividend" by retiring antiquated equipment, closing bases and downsizing Cold War infrastructure, and, in the case of the U.K. and France, reducing expenditures on nuclear weapons.

- A number of countries—notably Germany, France, Italy, the Netherlands, and Spain—have plans to eliminate or reduce conscription (which constrains the ability of European governments to send troops abroad) or increasingly rely on volunteers for the rapid reaction units they have created to carry out non–Article 5 missions.

- Major force structure changes have taken place (in the U.K. and the Netherlands) or are under way (in France, Italy, Spain, Turkey, and Greece). In each of these countries, albeit to varying degrees, forces are being reconfigured to perform the full spectrum of NATO missions, with increased emphasis on meeting the operational requirements of crisis management, humanitarian, and other peace support operations.

- The scope of German military commitments has slowly expanded, culminating in the deployment of German combat forces to the Stabilization Force (SFOR) in the former Yugoslavia and in the participation of German forces in Operation Allied Force in Kosovo. Germany has embarked on a major restructuring of its armed forces that will improve German capabilities to carry out new NATO and EU missions.[18] The German public's acceptance of the use of German combat troops outside Germany is one of the most significant developments in German security policy since the end of the Cold War.

- Under the aegis of the ESDP, the EU is well on its way to developing autonomous military capabilities to conduct EU-led crisis management and peacekeeping operations in Europe when "NATO as a whole" is not engaged.

- The European defense industry appears poised for a major round of streamlining and consolidation. Increased transatlantic defense mergers and joint ventures may even be possible, especially in light of the United States' recent reforms of its export

---

[18]Roger Cohen, "Germans Plan to Trim Army and Rely Less on the Draft," *New York Times*, May 24, 2000; and Joseph Fitchett, "European Combat Force Gets a Lift," *International Herald Tribune*, May 24, 2000.

control process and defense trade policies.[19] Progress in these areas could pave the way not only for closer transatlantic armaments cooperation but also for the more efficient use of defense resources to support European force restructuring and modernization.

If these trends continue, it will be increasingly difficult for many allies—including the U.K., France, Italy, Germany, the Netherlands, and Turkey—to opt out of non–Article 5 operations, especially those within Europe, by claiming that they lack the capabilities to make a significant contribution. In other words, future decisions by allied governments to participate in U.S.-led NATO operations beyond Europe will be conditioned to a much greater extent than in the past by strategic and political considerations. What does an examination of these key influences suggest about which allies are likely to contribute forces to protect energy supplies and under what circumstances?

As previously noted, the Strategic Concept shifts the focus of Alliance defense planning from fixed territorial defense against invasion to crisis management and other non–Article 5 missions. Nonetheless, for operations beyond Europe there is neither Alliance consensus on interests, aims, and policies nor a common assessment of regional challenges and appropriate responses.[20] Moreover, the thinking of most European countries differs from that of the United States with respect to the problem of energy security. Consequently, there is no consensus within the Alliance on the mission of ensuring access to energy supplies. For the foreseeable future, it is therefore unlikely that the Alliance will define the Persian Gulf, the Caspian, and North Africa as specific areas of NATO responsibility. The key reasons for this outlook are as follows:

---

[19]See Gordon Adams, "Shaping a Trans-Atlantic Defense Industry Agenda for 2001," *Defense News*, March 6, 2000. See also Anne Marie Squeo, "U.S. and German Officials to Discuss Defense Deals," *Wall Street Journal*, August 24, 1999.

[20]For a comprehensive and incisive discussion of differences in transatlantic perspectives on and policies toward the Middle East, see Philip Gordon, *The Transatlantic Allies and the Changing Middle East*, Adelphi Paper 322, London: International Institute for Strategic Studies, September 1998. See also François Heisbourg, "The United States, Europe, and Military Force Projection," in Robert D. Blackwill and Michael Sturmer (eds.), *Allies Divided*, Cambridge, MA: MIT Press, 1997, pp. 277–297.

- Most Europeans are less concerned than the United States about the likelihood and potential consequences of oil supply disruptions. In the European view, even if oil interruptions were to occur, they would likely be of limited duration and the long-term effects on oil price and availability would be manageable. Rather than invest substantial resources in developing power projection capabilities to combat threats that they believe are unlikely or of limited consequence, European governments generally prefer other measures—including diplomacy and economic engagement and the stockpiling of oil reserves—to alleviate concerns over energy security. Most European governments, moreover, believe that the energy security "problem" is not really a matter of access, since even rogue states sell oil on the international market. Unless other compelling national security interests are at stake, there is no basis for the belief that European governments would be prepared to go to war solely over the price of oil, even if prices escalated sharply, because they could well assume that market forces will eventually restore equilibrium.

- Some European countries believe that both Iraqi and Iranian conventional and NBC threats, including the threat of long-range ballistic missile attack, have been exaggerated and that the United States has overreacted to efforts on the part of both countries to reconstitute their military capabilities. Other European allies, while in general agreement with U.S. assessments of Iraqi and Iranian military threats, are more pessimistic than the United States that Iranian and Iraqi NBC ambitions can be thwarted and tend to be more pragmatic in dealing with the NBC problem in the Gulf; for example, many are more willing to accept the possibility that ridding Iran and Iraq of their NBC weapons is an unrealistic objective. In addition, many Europeans show greater understanding of Iran's security concerns and are thus more tolerant of its NBC ambitions. Consequently, many European governments are uncomfortable with what they see as an excessive U.S. preoccupation with NBC proliferation and fear that overly aggressive efforts to counter Iranian and Iraqi military capabilities will raise tensions and distort the West's security policy in the region. One important manifestation of these divergent perspectives is the greater willingness of some European countries (e.g., France) to support lucrative energy deals with Iran and Iraq even though the revenue generated from these projects could be used for NBC weapons development as well as conventional force modernization.

- There is a lingering fear, which finds expression in European warnings about a "global NATO," that the United States seeks to turn NATO into an arm of its global national security strategy and in so doing will drag Europe into conflicts that do not affect its vital interests.[21] Most European countries, for instance, are not especially worried that Iran and Iraq will use NBC weapons against NATO territory or NATO forces engaged in peacekeeping operations, and most are not planning to fight high-intensity wars in an NBC environment. Accordingly, most European governments prefer to rely primarily on deterrence and nonmilitary means to combat the NBC threat and will be far more reluctant than the United States to spend scarce resources to deal with this challenge.

- European governments generally do not see regional threats in military terms. Most believe that internal instability, rather than external aggression, poses the greatest challenge to the security of the Gulf Arab states as well as major energy producers in other regions. In particular, many European governments feel that the United States has paid too little attention to Saudi Arabia's economic problems and the resulting potential for political and social turmoil in the Kingdom; more broadly, they believe that the United States places too much emphasis on the military dimensions of regional security, arguing that diplomatic, economic, and political engagement is the most effective strategy for coping with the real challenges confronting the Gulf states.

- European governments generally believe that the United States relies too heavily on military force to resolve security problems. Thus, while some European governments might under some circumstances contribute militarily to the defense of Kuwait or Saudi Arabia against an unprovoked Iraqi or Iranian attack, they would be more cautious in responding militarily to more limited and ambiguous Iraqi and Iranian provocations. Moreover, with the exception of the U.K., most European governments are

---

[21]For two critical European perspectives, see Kamp, "A Global Role for NATO?" and Heisbourg, "New NATO, New Division of Labour."

deeply attached to the principle that their use of force, especially for non–Article 5 missions outside alliance territory, should be authorized by the United Nations Security Council (UNSC) and based firmly on international law. They are also more inclined than the United States to pursue political and economic measures to safeguard Western interests in the region. In short, the United States is prepared to contemplate the threat or use of force under a much wider range of circumstances than its European allies and is more inclined to undertake military operations unilaterally if necessary.

- Most European countries believe that U.S. policies in the Persian Gulf erode rather than enhance energy security. In particular, they have serious reservations about the U.S. policy of "dual containment," which seeks to isolate and punish Iran and Iraq as a means of influencing their behavior.[22] European governments instead favor a more conciliatory policy of engagement, which emphasizes positive inducements rather than "sticks" to promote cooperation with Iran and Iraq and encourage their integration into the international community. In the European view, the most effective way to moderate Iranian and Iraqi behavior and to ensure Western access to Gulf energy supplies is to develop strong ties with Iran and Iraq through expanded trade, dialogue, investment, and commerce. The European predilection for engagement with Iran has been reinforced by the recent success of the reform movement in moving Iran toward greater democratization and openness with the West. More fundamentally, European governments, with the exception of the U.K., do not share the stated U.S. goal of eliminating Saddam Hussein.

- Preserving energy security in the Persian Gulf would require a substantial increase in European power projection capabilities as well as improvements in the ability of European forces to operate in a WMD environment. Most allies are reluctant to commit substantial financial resources to make these improvements owing primarily to declining defense expenditures, the economic

---

[22]For a highly critical French critique of U.S. policy toward Iraq and "dual containment," see Eric Rouleau, "America's Unyielding Policy Toward Iraq," *Foreign Affairs*, Vol. 14, No. 1, January-February 1998, pp. 59–72.

imperatives of the Economic and Monetary Union (EMU), and burgeoning social demands on tight budgets.

• The different energy-producing regions are not all of equal importance to each member of the Alliance. Virtually all the allies see the Caspian as tangential to their core security and energy concerns, and none, with the possible exception of Turkey, is likely to become a major consumer or distributor of Caspian oil. Southern members of NATO see North Africa as at least equally important to their interests as the Gulf.

POLITICAL CONSTRAINTS ON COALITION OPERATIONS

Domestic and international political constraints are also likely to limit the availability of European forces for major military operations outside Europe. First and foremost, European governments generally face strong domestic political opposition to NATO military involvement in regions beyond Europe. Although they may take the notion seriously that NATO should extend security and stability throughout the Euro-Atlantic region, European publics are extremely wary of embarking on major combat operations in far-flung places beyond Europe. To overcome this opposition, European governments will have to convince skeptical publics that vital national or Western interests are at stake and that all diplomatic efforts to prevent conflict have been exhausted.

Second, the Strategic Concept papered over rather than resolved the "mandate" issue—i.e., whether NATO can undertake military action without a U.N. mandate. Most European governments would strongly prefer to have collective NATO military action outside Europe legitimized by some broader international mandate (e.g., the U.N. or the Organization for Security and Cooperation in Europe [OSCE]). In the absence of such authorization, some NATO countries may limit or refuse participation in coalition operations.

For the foreseeable future, it is therefore doubtful that there will be much public support in European countries for sending military forces outside Europe (other than on humanitarian or low-risk peacekeeping operations) except in very special circumstances. These conditions include a perception of a serious threat to vital national or Western interests; a UNSC mandate for military operations;

strong U.S. or EU leadership; and broad regional and international support for Western military intervention. While many NATO countries will support participation in low-risk peacekeeping and humanitarian operations within Europe, few are likely to contribute forces for major combat operations outside Europe, especially if these military commitments have the potential to become prolonged and costly.

Accordingly, European participation in coalition operations outside Europe will be circumscribed by numerous political constraints that will create wide disparities in the willingness and ability of European NATO members to contribute to energy security. Because of the fissures that would result from efforts to gain North Atlantic Council (NAC) approval of an Alliance military operation in the Gulf, allied military action is likely to be undertaken by so-called coalitions of the willing, as was the case during Operation Desert Storm. The key question, therefore, pivots on the conditions under which individual allied countries would be prepared to participate in military operations outside Europe as members of a multinational coalition. European countries are likely to subject decisions to participate in such coalitions of the willing to five key tests:

- The interests at stake are of sufficient importance to warrant the use of force.

- The political objectives of military operations are clear and public support is sustainable at the level of anticipated military casualties, collateral damage, and length of combat.

- There is a coherent and viable military strategy to achieve success.

- The costs and risks of military intervention are judged to be tolerable.

- The coalition is likely to be successful in achieving its objectives.

Clearly, these questions cannot be answered in the abstract, as much will depend on the nature of the threat, the specific contingencies where force might be required, and whether the United States exercises strong leadership. Nonetheless, as indicated in Figure 3.1, several general conclusions can be drawn:

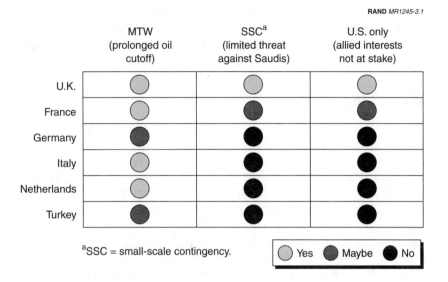

RAND *MR1245-3.1*

Figure 3.1—Allied Participation in Coalition Operations

- **Major theater war.** In response to large-scale, unprovoked Iraqi or Iranian aggression against key Gulf states, the United States can probably count on the U.K. to commit significant air, ground, and perhaps naval forces. If the UNSC has sanctioned Western military intervention, France is also likely to make a sizable contribution of combat forces, while other allies are likely to provide modest combat forces, combat support, combat service support, and basing/overflight rights. Without the UNSC's imprimatur, the military involvement of all allies, except Great Britain, is far more problematic.

- **Smaller-scale contingencies.** There is likely to be far less consensus on allied military participation in limited conflicts where the nature of the threat and the interests at stake are more ambiguous. In these scenarios, many of which are outlined in Chapter Two, the United States can probably depend only on the U.K. for a serious military contribution, with or without a UNSC mandate. In the absence of such a mandate, however, other allies, with the possible exception of France, are likely to rebuff

U.S. appeals for participation in coalition operations. In short, the United States will probably do most of the heavy lifting in the military contingencies it is most likely to confront in the Gulf over the next decade.

United Kingdom

As the strongest U.S. ally, the U.K. is likely to participate in combat operations beyond Europe if there is a threat to important Western interests, even in the absence of a U.N. mandate. The U.K. is the most outward-looking among the U.S. European allies and shares the U.S. strategic approach to NATO transformation. The U.K. is, in addition, restructuring its forces to operate beyond Europe. Future British governments, regardless of their political complexion, will place a high priority on maintaining and strengthening the U.K.'s "special relationship" with the United States. The U.K. also has abiding historical, political, and economic interests in the Persian Gulf, which are reflected in the emphasis that its *Strategic Defence Review* (SDR) places on developing the capability to project and sustain power in the Gulf and elsewhere. In short, the British will likely sustain their investment in high-quality armed forces trained, equipped, and structured for power projection and are likely to continue to make steady progress in rectifying the most serious deficiencies they face in their power projection capabilities.

France

France is likely to participate in combat operations beyond Europe if a clear threat is posed to vital Western interests. France is also investing substantially in improved expeditionary capabilities. Unlike the British, however, the French would press aggressively for a U.N. mandate; without one, French participation is far less likely.

France has a long tradition of defending its overseas commitments and interests when challenged, and the French have embarked on a program to create a credible power projection capability. Moreover, the French have extensive interests in the Arab world that would weigh heavily in any decision to use force in the Gulf, and the assertion of French power beyond Europe resonates in a country that seeks to play a larger role on the world stage. In particular, the

French have an important stake in Algerian gas and a historic commitment to the defense of Tunisia that could figure in energy-related military actions (e.g., security of the trans-Mediterranean pipeline). Indeed, gas supply is now the leading French concern in Algeria, and the French have been quietly keen on exploring the potential for U.S. participation in any Algerian contingencies. Because of France's proximity to Algeria, French power projection capabilities, although limited, could play an effective role.

At the same time, however, the French are opposed to an expansion of NATO's role beyond Europe, largely because they see such a focus as strengthening NATO—and U.S. domination of the Alliance—at the expense of the EU. Indeed, in contrast to the United States, the French believe that NATO's role in non–Article 5 operations outside Europe should be subject to a UNSC mandate. The French maintain that there is sound basis in international law for this position— notably Chapter VIII of the U.N. Charter—and that to flout it would set a dangerous precedent.

Germany

Germany has broken the post–World War II taboo on the deployment of German forces outside its borders. For historical, cultural, and political reasons, however, the German public is still skittish about German military operations beyond Europe. Moreover, the survival of a future German government, if that government is ruled by a Social Democratic Party/Green Coalition, could be threatened by German military action abroad that is unpopular at home. Simply put, German combat operations outside Europe will remain politically sensitive for many years to come and could sow serious divisions in the German body politic.

These considerations will impose important constraints on the scope of Germany's military commitments beyond Europe. Germany will continue to proceed cautiously and incrementally in improving its power projection capabilities and in removing inhibitions on the use of German forces outside German territory. Over the coming years, Germany will therefore remain most comfortable participating in non–Article 5 peacekeeping and humanitarian operations within Europe.

Indeed, throughout the Alliance debate last year on the Strategic Concept, Germany sought to limit the geographic scope of non–Article 5 operations—a stance reflecting the government's sensitivity to public neuralgia about NATO's role as a "global policeman." In addition, by restricting the scope of NATO's out-of-area operations, Germany hopes to avoid provoking a negative Russian reaction.[23] German forces are, moreover, largely configured to defend German territory and have a limited capability for power projection. As part of the defense review concluded in the spring of 2000, however, German forces are likely to undergo a significant downsizing and restructuring that will give them a greater power projection capacity.

Other factors will also push Germany to participate in military operations beyond Europe's borders, including the Gulf. Berlin will feel pressure to remain in step with its European partners, especially if there is an ESDP dimension to European military operations in the Gulf or if European forces are deployed in multinational formations that include German forces. Historically, Germany has sought to avoid isolation within the Alliance, and even the new postwar generation of more assertive and independent German leaders will feel the impulse to be "good Alliance citizens." In addition, the German government will be highly sensitive to the transatlantic aspects of coalition operations in the Persian Gulf and the impact that a decision to sit on the sidelines would have on U.S.-German relations in particular and U.S.-European relations in general.

Faced with these conflicting pressures, future German governments are likely to participate in coalition operations when (1) Germany perceives a serious threat to German or Western security interests; (2) the United States is exerting strong leadership and other allies, especially the U.K. and France, are in solidarity with the United States; and (3) there is strong international, regional, and domestic support for coalition operations. Of crucial importance to Germany will be whether the UNSC has authorized coalition operations and whether such operations are justified by international law. Thus, Germany will aggressively pursue a UNSC mandate for such operations should it decide to participate. If efforts to secure U.N. en-

---

[23]See Jacquelyn K. Davis and Charles M. Perry, *Report on European Issues and Developments,* Cambridge, MA: National Security Planning Associates, October 1998.

dorsement fail, however, German participation in military operations in the Persian Gulf would be highly questionable, and Berlin would cast about for other ways to offer its support.

Italy

Italian participation in combat operations beyond Europe is possible if there is a major threat to important Western interests, but only if sanctioned by a U.N. mandate. U.S. or NATO use of Italian bases in such operations would depend on several factors. If there is a European consensus to act, Italy would probably provide overflight rights and access to bases. Such access would be operationally important for North Africa and logistically important for the Gulf. Moreover, if the United States did not enjoy access to Suez, the burden on airlift—and regional allies to support airlift operations with bases—could increase enormously for Gulf contingencies. Sigonella rather than Aviano would be of central importance in this contingency, and the political constraints are much lower there.

Nonetheless, Italian involvement in military operations outside Europe should not be taken for granted. While Italy favors an expansion of NATO's role and is developing smaller, more modern, and better-trained armed forces for use in non–Article 5 contingencies, the focus of Italian security policy is the western Mediterranean and southeastern Europe. Moreover, although Italian participation in peacekeeping and humanitarian operations in these areas enjoys widespread public support, the deployment of forces in a hostile environment outside Europe would be far more controversial. Indeed, there is no consensus among the Italian public on American use of Italian bases to conduct military operations against Iraq. Continued U.S. and NATO use of Italian bases, for example, still arouses controversy among left-wing elements in the Italian political spectrum, many of whom see NATO as a Cold War relic and therefore question the expansion of its missions.[24] In sum, the Italian government would face a politically difficult decision to support Western military action outside Europe.

---

[24]Ibid.

Netherlands

The Dutch are likely to participate in coalition operations in the Gulf, but only under a U.N. umbrella and only if they perceive a significant threat to Western security interests. The Dutch contributed combat aircraft during Desert Storm and have strongly endorsed an expansion of the Alliance's missions. Indeed, during the debate on the Strategic Concept, the Netherlands argued that NATO preparedness to undertake non–Article 5 missions should be explicitly recognized as a core function of the Alliance.

In addition, there is strong support among the Dutch public for peacekeeping and humanitarian operations abroad, and the 1993 Defense Priorities Review shifted the emphasis of Dutch defense planning from the defense of NATO territory to the creation of more flexible and mobile forces suitable for rapid reaction and peacekeeping missions.[25] Nevertheless, the Dutch, like most other members of the Alliance, have serious reservations about extending NATO's reach beyond Europe, and it is unlikely that a political consensus will emerge to restructure Dutch forces for high-intensity combat operations outside Europe.

Spain

Like many other European allies, Spain is restructuring its military forces to increase its capability to contribute to multinational power projection missions. That said, Spain is unlikely to field forces capable of making a serious contribution in the Gulf. Spain's contribution to North African contingencies could be significant, however, and Spain could be a leading advocate for energy-related intervention to the south if its own gas supplies were threatened. Spanish bases could be very important for airlift and long-range strikes in Gulf contingencies (as in the use of Moron Air Base during the Gulf War; Rota could also be important for Middle Eastern airlift). The existence of a European consensus to participate with the United States will be the critical factor in determining Spain's approach and contribution.

---

[25]Ibid.

Turkey

Turkish support for coalition combat operations in the Gulf is unlikely unless Turkish territory or important Turkish interests are directly threatened. There are strong historical and political constraints against military involvement in the Middle East, especially within the Turkish military. Moreover, Turkey will be highly sensitive to the impact of any participation in Gulf contingencies on its relations with its regional neighbors in the Middle East and its access to energy. At the same time, the growing strength of Turkish nationalism, underscored by the strong showing of the Nationalist Action Party (MHP) in the April 1999 elections, makes use of Turkish facilities even more problematic, except when clear Turkish national interests are involved.

The outlook for Turkish participation will also be conditioned by other factors, including the growing centrality of energy access in Turkey's own security and prosperity. This reality could encourage a more interventionist approach on Ankara's part, especially in the case of direct, cross-border aggression (as in the Gulf War). In less clear-cut scenarios, Turkish civilian and military leaders will likely wish to avoid making enemies among suppliers and will be wary of actions that could threaten the security of, or revenue from, regional pipelines. Turkey will also be wary of taking any actions that could exacerbate the Kurdish problem or lead to the creation of a *de facto* Kurdish state in Northern Iraq.

In short, the readiness evinced by former Turkish President Türgut Özal during the Gulf War to allow the United States to use Turkish territory to launch attacks against Iraq is likely to be the exception rather than the rule. In the future, Turkey is likely to impose strong constraints on the use of its facilities, especially the air base at Incirlik, except in contingencies where Turkish interests are clearly threatened. It would therefore be unwise for U.S. military planners to assume that Turkish facilities will automatically be available in Middle Eastern or Persian Gulf contingencies.

FUTURE COALITION OPERATIONS

NATO's new Strategic Concept establishes a "road map" for extending stability and security throughout the Euro-Atlantic area. Many allies accept the need to develop improved capabilities for crisis management and humanitarian operations in Europe and to assume more of the military burden of meeting these challenges. Areas beyond Europe, however, fall outside this consensus.

Differences within NATO over strategy, policy, and interests in the Gulf, Caspian, and North Africa will likely preclude an Alliance consensus on joint military action to protect energy supplies. To some degree, these constraints will be shaped by the particular circumstances surrounding the threat. Indeed, according to one recent study, several trends underscore this point. First, more allies contribute a proportionately greater share of more diverse military assets in contingencies closer to home. Second, European countries have shown a distinct preference for participating in crisis management and peacekeeping operations rather than in MTW or major combat. Third, participation has varied greatly in both size and breadth from situation to situation.

The Persian Gulf

Unlike the Caspian and North Africa, most allies agree on the importance of preserving security in the Gulf and share a common interest in maintaining access to Gulf energy resources. Nonetheless, as previously noted, views differ over the nature of regional challenges to Western interests and the most effective means for responding to these threats. In addition, some allied countries, especially Germany and France, are adverse to a formal NATO role in the region.

Thus, a consensus within NATO has yet to crystallize on a common response to Saddam Hussein's challenge to the U.N. inspections regime in Iraq and his continued development of NBC weapons—both of which, at least from a U.S. perspective, constitute a clear threat to Western interests in the Persian Gulf. Indeed, sharp differences among the allies on policy toward Iran and Iraq underscore the absence of a common conception of interests and aims that could provide a solid underpinning to cooperation on power projection operations.[26]

---

[26]Heisbourg, "The United States, Europe, and Military Force Projection."

In the future, the prospect of joint allied military action in the Persian Gulf is therefore likely to arouse intense controversy within NATO. This is likely to be the case even under the best of circumstances—namely unprovoked, large-scale Iraqi or Iranian aggression that is clearly perceived as a serious threat to Western security interests and has been subjected to UNSC action and censured by the international community. Under these conditions, the U.K., France, Italy, and the Netherlands are likely to contribute combat forces, while German and Turkish participation would be more questionable. However, in the event of more ambiguous challenges, where the threat is less serious and allied interests are not perceived to be directly involved, the willingness of the countries above to participate in coalition operations is far more problematic. The United States could probably count only on the U.K. across the full spectrum of coalition contingencies, regardless of whether a coalition of like-minded countries is operating under a UNSC mandate.[27]

North Africa

A few southern members of the Alliance—notably France, Italy, Spain, and Portugal—have a strong interest in maintaining peace and stability in the Maghreb and in preserving access to the region's oil and, especially, gas resources. However, the interests of other allies, including the United States, are far less engaged. It is doubtful, for example, that any U.S. administration would be prepared to commit combat forces in Algeria or Libya in response to a cutoff of their energy supplies to southern Europe. That said, the United States might have difficulty turning aside a European request to intervene—or, more likely, provide assets for a European-led intervention.

In any event, those European countries that depend most heavily on North African oil and gas imports are skeptical of NATO military involvement in the region. Their preferred long-term strategy is to use political and economic instruments rather than military force to thwart the primary threats emanating from the region, including mi-

---

[27]For a discussion of NATO's future role outside Europe and especially in the Persian Gulf, see Michael Brown, "A Minimalist NATO," *Foreign Affairs*, Vol. 78, No. 3, May-June 1999, p. 210.

gration, terrorism, and Islamic fundamentalism. Consequently, they see this as a task best left to the "soft power" of the EU. Likewise, in a crisis, they are likely to see safeguarding North African energy supplies as a task for the future EU Rapid Reaction Force or possibly a European-led CJTF. France would oppose NATO military involvement in North Africa. In short, southern European countries are unlikely to urge NATO to plan and prepare for operations in the Maghreb. Accordingly, in response to a serious disruption of North African natural gas exports to southern Europe, the United States (and other NATO members) might face requests to approve the formation of an EU-led CJTF, to allow such an organization to use NATO assets, or to provide this coalition with essential combat support (C^{4}ISR).

The Caspian

With the exception of Turkey, the European allies see the Caspian as peripheral to their security. None would deem the independence of any of the major energy-producing states or continued access to Caspian energy as vital Western interests. Furthermore, while some European countries seek access to the region's energy resources, Caspian oil and gas do not play a major role in their energy diversification plans.

It would be extremely difficult for NATO to devise a common approach to security challenges in the region because of divergent views and threat perceptions. Most European countries do not see the Caspian in military terms and are likely to stress the use of "soft power" to cope with regional problems. Moreover, many NATO allies harbor serious fears that projecting force into the region would provoke a hostile Russian reaction. Put simply, the United States, assuming it decided that preserving access to Caspian oil was a vital interest, would face strong resistance to NATO military operations in the region. Only Turkey and possibly the U.K. might be willing to participate in such an operation.[28]

---

[28]For a comprehensive discussion of NATO's approach toward Caspian security, see Richard Sokolsky and Tanya Charlick-Paley, *NATO and Caspian Security: A Mission Too Far?* RAND, MR-1074-AF, 1999.

Indeed, if the United States or NATO were so inclined, the opening of the Caspian region to outside influence presents new opportunities for greater security cooperation with Turkey. Energy security figures importantly in Turkey's national security calculations. Ankara wants energy security to be part of an improved strategic relationship with the West and is eager to expand its influence in the Caspian region.

Turkey is therefore well positioned to play a unique role in facilitating Western power projection into the Caspian (and the Gulf) and is moving toward developing an independent power projection capability. Indeed, if the Baku-Ceyhan pipeline becomes a reality, the United States and its other NATO allies may face the prospect of deepening Turkish military involvement in the Caspian region that could result in a de facto or de jure Turkish commitment to defend oil pipelines. Under these circumstances, the possibility cannot be ruled out that Ankara might seek NATO cover and/or U.S. and NATO military assistance to fulfill these commitments.

IMPLICATIONS FOR MILITARY PLANNING

For nearly four decades, beginning with the Suez Crisis in 1956 and culminating most recently in the West's divided stance against Iraqi belligerence in the Persian Gulf, NATO has failed to develop and implement a coherent collective approach to security problems in SWA. The failure to achieve an Alliance-wide consensus on security measures in the region and a formal commitment to collective military planning and operations reflects differences not only between the United States and Europe but also among the Europeans themselves. Indeed, in some cases intra-European differences, be they political, geographic, or historical, have been as pronounced as, if not more pronounced than, transatlantic divisions.

NATO's failure as an institution to develop a common approach to the defense of SWA does not stem primarily from a lack of common interests or the absence of serious threats to those interests. Both Europe and the United States share a strong common interest in secure oil. Furthermore, over the past 20 years the West has confronted several significant threats to regional security, including the Soviet invasion of Afghanistan, the Iranian revolution, the Iran-Iraq War, the Gulf War, and Saddam Hussein's repeated challenges to post–Desert Storm UNSC resolutions.

In each of these situations, the Alliance was able to reach a fragile consensus on a politically acceptable resolution to avoid cracks in NATO unity. However, these solutions were weighted toward the lowest common denominator and thus fell far short of addressing the West's strategic vulnerability in SWA. From the European perspective, success was defined primarily in terms of limiting damage to transatlantic relations rather than producing major improvements in Alliance power projection capabilities for military operations outside Europe.

Amid the fault lines that have emerged in the Alliance debate on the out-of-area issue, the predominant view among European allies has been that military planning and operations for non–Article 5 missions beyond Europe should be conducted through bilateral and multilateral arrangements outside the Alliance framework. It was precisely for this reason that allied governments rebuffed the U.S. effort in the early 1980s to formalize a NATO out-of-area strategy for SWA—a view that was affirmed repeatedly over the past two decades and that is unlikely to be challenged for the foreseeable future.

The reasons for European opposition to an institutional role for NATO in SWA are deeply rooted in Europe's political consciousness and are therefore unlikely to change in the security environment the Alliance will confront over the next decade. A key factor is lack of domestic support for the use of force outside Europe. European governments also fear that NATO military operations outside Europe would undermine the Alliance's cohesion, European efforts to develop an independent voice in defense matters, and European freedom of action. Some European allies, notably France, are concerned that extending NATO's security commitments to SWA would perpetuate U.S. domination of the Alliance. Finally, a NATO role in the Gulf is hampered by persistent U.S.-European disagreements over the most effective means of protecting Western security interests and by divergent policies and perspectives on regional security issues.

Moreover, even if the United States consults closely with the European allies and is sensitive to European concerns, decisions by individual allies to commit combat forces in coalition operations to defend energy supplies will depend largely on the nature of the contingency and judgments about the costs, benefits, and risks of military intervention in the particular circumstances at hand. Thus, while the United States will face strong political imperatives to operate in a coalition, U.S. military planners will face the prospect, however unsatisfying, of ad hoc decisions by individual European countries to participate, on a case-by-case basis, in a coalition operation among like-minded NATO countries. The prospects are slim that the Alliance would ever approve a NATO military operation outside Europe.

In short, the United States will continue to encounter resistance from most European countries (with the exception of the U.K. and France) to improving their long-range power projection capabilities for high-intensity military operations outside Europe. As a result, while some European forces are likely to perform more effectively in a future Gulf war, it is unrealistic for the United States to depend on NATO's European members to pick up a significantly larger share of the burden of defending Western security interests in the Persian Gulf.

Chapter Four
ALLIED POWER PROJECTION CAPABILITIES
John E. Peters, David Shlapak, and Timothy Liston

As indicated in Chapter Two, U.S. and allied forces must be capable of responding to a broad range of contingencies that could threaten vital Western energy supplies. This chapter assesses European power projection capabilities, focusing particularly on the deployment of air power for major combat operations.[1] The first section discusses current allied air forces' capabilities. The second section describes allied plans to improve their air forces' power projection prowess. The third section assesses the adequacy of current and planned capabilities against the demands of the major combat operations described in Chapter Two. The final section examines possible allied contributions in contingencies short of an MTW.

CURRENT CAPABILITIES

The first question often posed about allied power projection is how many aircraft the allies can muster. The recent history of collective

---

[1]The discussion here first presumes that the allies commit to the formation of an Air Expeditionary Force (AEF) and then considers their prospects for success given current and planned air force capabilities. It cannot be emphasized too strongly, however, that embracing the AEF concept would be a major undertaking for any of the allies and would have huge implications for their planning, training, logistics, weapons procurement, and command arrangements. In addition, the closely coordinated and tightly interdependent activities of a multinational AEF would require the participating air forces to develop much closer habits of cooperation. Thus, while a move toward the AEF notion would be a welcome one, the difficulties inherent in such a move should not be underestimated. That said, the chapter couches its examination of current and future European air power potential in the framework of an AEF.

allied air operations suggests that a reasonable assessment of the size and quality of allied contributions for any given contingency will be influenced by a number of factors. Some countries have deployed more aircraft or responded more quickly than their answers to the NATO Defense Planning Questionnaire (DPQ) indicated. In contrast, the last time a serious challenge to energy supplies arose in the Middle East—an event that could reasonably have been expected to generate a large allied response, since it affected allied interests directly—few NATO allies committed air forces to direct combat. Only France, Italy, and the United Kingdom did so,[2] deploying 107 fighters and fighter-bombers along with 13 support aircraft.[3] At the same time, in operations such as Deliberate Forge, the air component of the Stability Force in Bosnia, the Europeans contributed up to 96 of the 124 aircraft involved.[4] In short, many Europeans have adopted a "coalition of the willing" approach, contributing forces to some operations out of a sense of being good European citizens, contributing to others for more compelling security considerations, and in still other instances demurring. Thus, the most useful way to gauge current European capabilities is to examine the recent record of deployments with the assumption that if the political will coalesces for air expeditionary operations, the contributions of the European allies will probably fall within a range reflected in their recent operational histories.

Operation Desert Shield/Desert Storm

When Iraq invaded Kuwait on August 2, 1990, America's European allies responded slowly and unevenly. The United Kingdom was among the first to reply, announcing Operation Granby on August 9. With this announcement, Britain began deploying its air forces: a squadron of Tornado F-3 fighters and a squadron of Jaguar ground attack aircraft. These squadrons were operational in the Kuwaiti

---

[2]For a complete description of the allied role in Operation Desert Storm, see Peters and Deshong, *Out of Area or Out of Reach?*

[3]U.S. Air Force, *Gulf War Air Power Survey*, Vol. 5, Table 14, Washington, D.C., 1993, pp. 48–50.

[4]Allied Forces South Public Information Office, "SFOR Air Component Fact Sheet," http://www.afsouth.nato.int/FACTSHEETS/SFORAirComponent.htm.

theater 48 hours later. Then, on August 23, London deployed a squadron of Tornado GRR-1 aircraft.

The French and Italian military responses were somewhat more deliberate. Paris began initial deployments in late August, principally of naval, helicopter, and ground force elements. France committed combat air forces only after Iraq seized the French ambassador's residence in Kuwait on September 14. Italy deployed its air force component in September. Table 4.1 summarizes allied air force contributions to this effort.

By contrast, the U.S. force contribution dwarfed that of the Europeans. In addition to deploying roughly 1300 combat aircraft, the U.S. contributed 308 tankers, 149 transport aircraft, and 29 specialized planes ranging from reconnaissance to battle management. The U.S. contribution was also significantly larger than that of the Europeans in another critical respect: stockpiles of air force munitions in the theater of operations. Prior to Operation Desert Storm, the U.S. Air Force had 48,325 short tons of munitions pre-positioned in the region.[5]

Operation Allied Force

The most recent example of allied air operations—Operation Allied Force, conducted against Serbia—began on March 24, 1999, and

Table 4.1

**NATO Contributions of Air Forces in
Desert Storm**

Country	Fighter/Bomber	Support
Canada	18	—
France	32	6
Italy	8	—
U.K.	49	7
U.S.	1317	486
Totals	1424	499

SOURCE: U.S. Air Force, *Gulf War Air Power Survey*, Vol. 5, Table 14, 1993.

---

[5]U.S. Air Force, *Gulf War Air Power Survey*, Vol. 3, p. 224.

ended on June 20, 1999. The military objective of this effort was
". . . to degrade and damage the military and security structure that
President Milosevic [Yugoslav president] has used to depopulate and
destroy the Albanian majority in Kosovo."[6]

All 19 NATO members contributed to that objective, and 13 of them
flew missions in the air campaign. The United States and the allies
deployed some 770 and 275 aircraft, respectively. The allied contribution included 192 fighter-bombers, 63 support aircraft, 19 reconnaissance aircraft, and three helicopters.[7] In addition, France and
Britain both operated an aircraft carrier in the area. Table 4.2 lists
the numbers and types of aircraft contributed by key allies.

The deployment decision process developed over a period of several
months, so Allied Force was not a test of prompt deployment. The

Table 4.2

Aircraft Contributions from Key Allies

France	Germany	Italy	Netherlands	U.K.
6 Jaguar	14 Tornado	12 Tornado ECR/IDS[a]	14 F-16AM	3 E-3D
4 Mirage F1CR	1 C-160	6 AMX	6 F-16	16 Harrier GR-7
11 Mirage 2000C		6 F-104 ASA		1 Canberra PR-9
7 Mirage 2000D		6 Tornado IDS		4 L-1011
1 C-160		4 Tornado ECR/IDS		12 Tornado
3 KC-135		4 F-104 ASA		5 VC-10
1 Mirage IV-P		1 Boeing 707T		7 Sea Harrier FFA-2[b]
1 E-3F SDCA				10 Sea King
14 Super Etendard				
4 Etendard IVP[b]				
4 Super Frelon				
56	15	39	20	58

SOURCE: http://www.stratfor.com/crisis/kosovo/natoorderofbattle.htm.

[a]ECR = electronic combat and reconnaissance; IDS = interdiction and strike.

[b]Indicates carrier-based aircraft.

---

[6]"Operation Allied Force Fact Sheet," at http://www.defenselink.mil/specials/
kosovo/index.html.

[7]Ibid.

NAC issued the activation order on October 13, 1998. On January 20, 1999, NATO decided to increase the readiness of the assigned forces so that they would be able to execute an operation on 48 hours' notice. Further instructions increasing readiness were issued nine days later. On March 22, in response to Belgrade's continued intransigence, the NAC authorized the UNSC to decide on a broad range of air operations should they become necessary. Air operations began two days later.

Figure 4.1 summarizes the allied sorties flown in Operation Allied Force and Operation Deliberate Force. Owing to Kosovo's demanding topographical conditions, strict rules of engagement, and poor weather conditions, a premium was placed on PGMs and on aircraft that could support the strike sorties flown by NATO. Of the 38,000 sorties flown, 27 percent were strike and 73 percent support sorties.[8] (Strike sorties are those actually designated to drop munitions on targets; support sorties are all others involved in the air campaign.) The allies flew a considerable number of strike sorties, comprising 47 percent of the total—but that overstates their contribution. Of the sorties that required precision strike or that took place in adverse weather conditions, a disproportionate number were flown by the United States.[9] Of the 23,614 air munitions released by NATO aircraft, more than 30 percent were PGMs.[10] This represents a sharp increase over the amount dropped in the Persian Gulf War, where the proportion of PGMs was only 10 percent of the total dropped. There is every reason to believe that this proportion will increase further in future conflicts. The number of PGMs dropped by the European allies was only 7 percent of the overall total, reflecting a shortfall in these types of weapons among the Europeans.

---

[8]United Kingdom Ministry of Defence Web site, http://www.mod.uk/news/Kosovo/account/stats/htm.

[9]William S. Cohen, July 20, 1999, at http://www.defenselink.mil/dodgc/lrs/docs/test07-20-99Cohen.html.

[10]United Kingdom Ministry of Defence Web site, "Account of the Crisis—Operation Allied Force: NATO Air Campaign in FRY," http://www.mod.uk/news/kosovo/account/stats.htm.

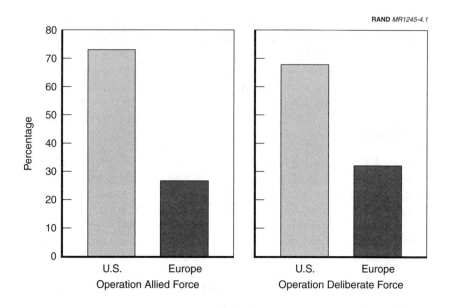

Figure 4.1—Sorties Flown in Operation Allied Force and Operation Deliberate Force

Another important component of Operation Allied Force was the support element. Tankers, electronic warfare, surveillance and reconnaissance, and forward air control–capable aircraft were depended on heavily in each stage of the air operations. However, the European allies' lack of capabilities in jamming, refueling, and intelligence, surveillance, and reconnaissance (ISR) meant that the bulk of support missions were carried out by the United States; indeed, of the approximately 27,000 support sorties flown during Operation Allied Force, slightly more than 70 percent were flown by the United States.[11] There were, however, exceptions to this rule. For example, the allies did contribute a good number of capable unmanned aerial vehicles (UAVs) and, as mentioned above, fighter aircraft to the operation. But the lack of advanced munitions and of specialized support aircraft marginalized the allies' contribution to the air war over Yugoslavia.

---

[11]Cohen, statement to the Senate Armed Services Committee.

NATO has also been conducting other peace operations in the Balkans and elsewhere. Table 4.3 summarizes the size of the aircraft contributions to some of these operations for key allies. As this figure shows, the collective aircraft contribution from these allies ranged from 49 aircraft for Deliberate Forge to 163 aircraft for Deliberate Force. France's average contribution was about 27 aircraft; Germany's was 14, Italy's 17, and the Netherlands' 13. The average contribution from Spain, Turkey, and the United Kingdom was 9, 11, and 19, respectively. The expeditionary air force elements sought from European air forces to assist in a Middle East halt phase are within the scope of the forces generated by these allied forces during Operation Allied Force.

Precision Munitions

European air forces must be able to arm their aircraft with effective munitions, and in recent years this has come to mean having PGMs.

Table 4.3

Aircraft Contributions of Selected Allies

Country	Deny Flight	Deliberate Force	Decisive Endeavor	Deliberate Guard	Deliberate Forge
France	33	50	20	24	6
Germany	14	14	18	16	7
Italy	20	24	16	15	11
Netherlands	15	18	11	12	8
Spain	11	11	7	11	6
Turkey	8	18	8	18	4
U.K.	28	28	12	18	7
Total	129	163	92	114	49

SOURCE: Compiled from NATO and AFSOUTH fact sheets and *The Military Balance 1998/99,* London: International Institute for Strategic Studies, 1998. Deny Flight is an ongoing enforcement operation, maintaining a no fly zone over Bosnia-Herzegovina. Deliberate Force constituted the largest air assault in the history of NATO up to that time. The Alliance conducted air operations in response to the 1995 shelling of the Sarajevo central marketplace by the Bosnian Serb Army. Decisive Endeavor was the air component of the Implementation Force (IFOR) in Bosnia. Deliberate Guard was the air element of the Stability Force, the successor to IFOR. Deliberate Forge was the predecessor operation to Allied Force over Kosovo and Serbia.

Three main factors have shaped European decisions regarding the acquisition of precision munitions. First, NATO force goals encouraged the allies to buy ordnance suitable for the defense of the Central Region against a Warsaw Pact attack. Rolling terrain punctuated by forests, villages, cities, and mountains often provided good cover and concealment, making it difficult to engage point targets. Area munitions, including scatterable mines and cluster bombs, were appropriate in that they could exploit the terrain to create choke points in valleys, at bridges, and in front of towns that would disrupt the enemy's advance.

Second, anticipating that any conventional war would quickly escalate to tactical nuclear weapons or worse, many European governments bought only the minimum essential conventional munitions. If the war was going to escalate after only a few weeks of conventional fighting, the European allies questioned the value of maintaining large stocks of conventional munitions. As a result, at the height of the Cold War some allied countries maintained stocks adequate for only 15 days.

Third, the effectiveness of precision munitions developed gradually from the Vietnam era to the present, making spectacular strides in the early 1990s. These munitions were slow to gain prominence in Europe, however, especially since the NATO force goals did not require large stocks of them. Although some countries acquired small stocks of laser-guided weapons (e.g., the AGM-65 Maverick, the Paveway, and the French AS-30L), most arsenals continued to feature cluster munitions and unguided iron bombs.

As a result of these factors, only eight of the 13 air forces that flew in Operation Allied Force carried precision munitions, and then in only limited quantities.[12] Table 4.4 offers a snapshot of the limited employment of such weapons in Deliberate Force, the operation that preceded Allied Force.

---

[12]Kenneth R. Bacon and Thomas Wilson, DoD news briefing, Apri 30, 1999, reported at http://www.defenselink.mil/news/Apr1999/t04301999_t0430asd.html.

Table 4.4

Precision Munitions in Operation Deliberate Force

Country	Precision	Nonprecision	HARM[a]
France	14	73	
Germany			
Italy		50	
Netherlands		136	
Spain	24		2
Turkey			
U.K.	48	47	
U.S.	622	12	54
Total	708	318	56

SOURCE: Compiled by Eric Larson from Robert C. Owen et al., *Deliberate Force: A Case Study in Effective Air Campaigning,* Maxwell AFB, AL: School of Advanced Airpower Studies, June 1998.

[a]HARM = High-Speed Antiradiation Missile.

Key allies' exact holdings in precision munitions are currently uncertain because of recent operations against Serbian forces and because several countries have given vague answers about their inventories to the DPQ. Nonetheless, publicly available budgets and acquisition documents suggest that several countries' inventories number only in the hundreds. In contrast, the U.S. plans to procure 90,000 Joint Direct Attack Munitions (JDAMs)—one of only several PGMs in the inventory.[13]

Long-Range Deployment

The primary question about long-range deployment is whether the allies have the means to move their AEFs to the theater of operations. Aircraft that can refuel in flight can self-deploy out to the limits of the pilot's endurance; others are dependent on intermediate air bases. A key consideration is the adequacy of plans and capabilities to ensure that critical support personnel and equipment are in place.

United Kingdom. In the U.K., 27 VC-10 tankers support transport and refueling operations. Some 50 C-130 aircraft provide long-range

---

[13]Bacon and Wilson, DoD news briefing, April 30, 1999.

transport, although some Tristars and Bae 111s are also available.[14] In addition, Britain has signed an agreement with France for a Franco-British Euro Air Group (FBEAG), a planning and coordination cell with no aircraft assigned that could designate, on a case-by-case basis, the best aircraft units of the two countries—combat or transport—to participate in operations and exercises. The cell provides a framework for combined operations that could be conducted bilaterally or under charter from the WEU.[15]

The Readiness of Royal Air Force (RAF) aircraft is at present a controversial issue. A recent Ministry of Defence report indicated that only about half the Tornadoes, Harriers, and Jaguars can be battle ready in less than a week. Only eight of 21 Nimrod aircraft considered in the report were found to be ready for operations. Although the RAF has disputed these claims,[16] low readiness rates for RAF units are consistent with the lower readiness of British naval and ground forces and with the explicit policies of the Ministry of Defence.[17]

France. Like the United States, France has organized the majority of its air forces into an air combat command and an air mobility command.[18] The air mobility command operates 13 transport squadrons, an electronic warfare squadron, and six helicopter squadrons. The transport squadrons include one heavy squadron flying DC-8F and Airbus A310-300 aircraft, five tactical squadrons based principally on C-160 aircraft but supplemented with some C-130s, and seven light transport squadrons operating an assortment of C-160s, DHC-6s, CN-235s, and other aircraft.[19] The air force has withdrawn from the future large aircraft program, and no new

---

[14]*The Military Balance 1998/99.*

[15]WEU Assembly, "Report on European Armed Forces," WEU Document 1468, June 12, 1995.

[16]Andrew Buncombe, "Half of RAF's Warplanes Unfit to Fly," *London Independent,* July 24, 1998, p. 6.

[17]Comments by Mr. Jon Day, Director of Defence Policy in the Ministry of Defence, RAND, August 5, 1998.

[18]*The Military Balance 1998/99.*

[19]Ibid.

strategic airlift acquisitions are likely to occur in the next four to five years.[20]

Germany. In addition to its 87 C-160 transports, the German Air Force (Luftwaffe) relies on "market aircraft"—i.e., those that can be contracted off the economy—to help it deploy major elements. Several options are now under consideration for expanding airlift range and capacity, among which are leasing IL-76 and Antonov 24 aircraft from Russia and the Ukraine. Perhaps the most innovative option would involve leasing 100 hours of flight time annually for Airbus A300-600ST "Beluga" giant transports. The Luftwaffe has master agreements with charter carriers "under agreement" but thus far has none in place.[21] The German Air Force has no tankers for in-flight refueling, although current plans call for the conversion of some transports to transport-tanker configurations.[22]

Italy. The Italian Air Force's long-range transportation capabilities currently reside in its Transport and Rescue Command. The command operates 36 G-222 and 12 C-130H U.S.-built transports and is taking delivery of at least 18 C-130J aircraft. The command also operates four Boeing 707-328 tankers and two 707-328Bs in logistics configuration.[23]

Netherlands. The Royal Netherlands Air Force operates two tankers and 19 assorted C-130-size transports and maritime patrol aircraft. Otherwise, the service operates 13 CH-47D large transport helicopters and 43 utility helicopters.

Spain. Spain's transport and logistics forces have been undergoing modernization since 1994. The air force's long-range transportation assets include 56 C-212 medium transports, seven C-130s, six tankers of various models, and two each Boeing 707-320C and CN-235 transports.[24]

---

[20] Ibid.

[21] Ibid.

[22] Ibid.

[23] *USNI Periscope Database,* Nation's Armed Forces Database, February 1, 1999, http://www.periscope.ucg.com/.

[24] *USNI Periscope Database,* January 1, 1999.

Table 4.5 summarizes the major aircraft contributing to each country's long-range reach. In some instances, aircraft are dual-use, serving as both transports and tankers. Recalling that Operation Allied Force required only 63 support aircraft to sustain the allied contribution to the air campaign against Serbia, the pool of available transport and tanker aircraft, provided they had adequate access to forward basing, is adequate to support up to two allied AEFs. The transport and tanker inventory is sufficient, especially in instances such as Operation Allied Force, in which there is no requirement to deploy ground forces. Under such circumstances, all of the transport and tanker assets could be devoted to supporting the deploying air forces. That said, it should be noted that Operation Desert Storm required 222 USAF tankers for in-theater support and another 86 outside the area of responsibility (AOR). If future operations required disproportionately larger tanker contributions from the allies, most would have great difficulties satisfying them.

Forward Basing and Force Protection

Once the air forces deploy to the crisis region, questions of basing and force protection move to the fore. Basing issues have to do with how much base support infrastructure the allies can bring along to sustain their forces. Force protection issues center on the allies' ability to protect their forward-deployed units from a range of threats, including NBC, conventional military, and terrorist attacks.

Basing Requirements. Unlike the USAF, which can import the base operating systems and infrastructure its deployed units require, the

Table 4.5

**Major Transport and Tanker Aircraft of
Selected Allies**

Country	Transports	Tankers
France	98	28
Germany	87	0
Italy	68	4
Netherlands	19	2
Spain	67	6
U.K.	50	27
Total	389	67

European allies are more dependent on fully developed airfields to support their operations. Their operational effectiveness depends to a large degree on the availability of modern airfields with a full suite of facilities for crews, aircraft, and support personnel. Although some of the allies—i.e., Britain, France, and Italy—have limited airfield development capabilities, none has the ability to develop austere airfields fully on short notice.[25] Typical capabilities include airborne engineers trained to parachute in to a remote site and carve out a landing strip. However, this level of capacity pales in comparison to U.S. Air Force Red Horse construction capabilities, which can quickly extend runways, create new ramp space, build fuel and ammunition storage, and perform other related tasks.

Force Protection. Any country deploying military forces to the Persian Gulf must reckon with a variety of threats. Even air forces, which are based well beyond the reach of enemy armor and artillery, must be prepared for attacks by missiles, aircraft, truck bombers, and NBC weapons.

Each of the principal allies has some capabilities that contribute to force protection, but even their collective capabilities produce a vulnerable shield. Based on the Operation Allied Force experience, the allies could mass some 190 fighter-bombers for an offensive counterair operation to destroy enemy air forces. In addition, all of the allies can deploy low- and medium-altitude air defense systems to protect against air attack by enemy fighters, and the Dutch have Patriot batteries for high-altitude defense. Moreover, all of the allies could deploy ground forces to improve security against truck bombs and terrorist attacks, and some, especially the British, have excellent human intelligence (HUMINT) that could improve security by creating a warning network to alert their forces to a coming attack. Finally, all of the allies can provide their forces with basic NBC training and individual protective equipment.

None of the allies, however, can provide either a reliable theater missile defense over their forward-deployed units or the "survive-to-operate" (STO) systems necessary to protect their forces from NBC

---

[25]Italy, for example, maintains a parachute engineer company for this task. The British RAF maintains some capability in the ground squadrons of the air force regiment. Others draw on army resources.

attack (e.g., protective shelters and decontamination equipment for aircraft and their support systems). Allied air defense systems, for example, are intended to engage enemy aircraft, not incoming missiles. In short, none of the allies currently have STO systems to support AEFs in a foreign theater for sustained military operations.

Effective Military Operations

Effective military operations depend on many factors. For AEFs, the critical questions include:

- Once in the theater of operations, can the air forces generate enough sorties to contribute to the campaign's objectives?

- Do the air forces have the right ordnance to attack critical targets?

- Can all the air forces make use of the same command and control system, share air tasking orders (ATOs), and coordinate effectively among national contingents?

Generating Sorties

Two key allies, France and the United Kingdom, have released some details of their armed forces' respective roles in Operation Allied Force that can assist in drawing conclusions about military effectiveness. France contributed 88 aircraft to the operation. The French Air Force flew 45 fighter-bombers, six tankers, two airborne early warning (AEW) and command-and-control aircraft, three combat search and rescue (CSAR) helicopters, nine reconnaissance aircraft, and one C-160 Transall transport. The naval carrier air group embarked for the operation included 16 Super Etendard fighter-bombers, four reconnaissance aircraft, and two CSAR helicopters. According to the French Ministry of Defense, the allies flew roughly 10,450 offensive sorties, of which France flew 1261, or 12 percent. Of the 1564 reconnaissance missions flown over Serbia and Kosovo, French forces flew 330, or 21 percent.[26]

---

[26]Ministère de la Défense, *Lessons from Kosovo: Analysis and References*, Paris, November 1999.

Britain has also detailed the size of the air forces it deployed for Allied Force. According to data released by the British Ministry of Defence, by the end of the operation Britain had flown 1,008 or almost 10 percent of the approximately 10,450 bombing sorties that the Alliance had carried out. The British also helped support the offensive sorties. Over the course of Allied Force, British planes flew 102 Combat Air Patrol, 184 AEW, and 324 air-to-air refueling (AAR) sorties.[27]

These sortie rates would be a major contribution toward the 1300 to 1600 sorties that some modeling results suggest would be necessary to halt a six-division armored force attacking into Saudi Arabia. The allies might in fact fare better in a desert campaign, where there would be few innocent civilians to worry about and where cluster munitions could still contribute significantly to stopping the armored onslaught. If there were fewer constraints on munitions and opportunities to use other types of ordnance, the principal allies might generate even more combat sorties.

Appropriate Ordnance

Table 4.6 shows selected acquisitions of precision munitions. Most of the allies have programs under way to develop new munitions, but many such programs are not mature enough to provide a reliable indication of how many will ultimately be produced. Another area of uncertainty that clouds judgment about whether the allies will have appropriate ordnance in sufficient numbers for halt-phase operations has to do with the prospects for converting "dumb bombs." In many instances, unguided ordnance can be adapted by adding a guidance kit to the nose and a "tail kit" to provide steerage. For countries like Britain and Germany, which share some common ordnance with the United States (e.g., MK-82 bombs), the prospects for upgrading older bombs are good; they need only buy the modification kits. For other countries, however—including France, whose 2000-kg bomb is not compatible with U.S. modification kits—alternative options must be pursued. Stocks of other ordnance are important as well, especially those located in the theater of operations.

---

[27]Douglas Henderson and Sir John Day, briefing, June 11, 1999, reported at http://www.mod.uk/news/kosovo/brief110699.htm.

Table 4.6

Selected Acquisitions of Precision Munitions

Weapon Name	Purchasing Country	Number Acquired	Date of Acquisition
AGM-65	Germany	1400	1988
Maverick	Italy	42	1994
AGM-88	Germany	944	1991
HARM	Spain	80	1990
	Italy	564	1992
	Turkey	50	1993
	Netherlands	0	
ALARM[a]	U.K.	750	1983
		200	1992
Scalp	France	300	1998
AS.30L	France	1172	1998
TADS/Taurus[b]	Germany	600	2007
	Italy	200	2007
AGM-114 Brimstone	U.K.	700	2006
AASM "smart bomb"	France	250	2007
BGL[c] laser-guided bomb	France	425	1997

SOURCE: Teal Group Corporation, *World Missiles Briefing*, Greenwich, CT, 1999.

[a]ALARM = air-launched antiradiation missile.

[b]TADS = target-adaptive dispenser system.

[c]BGL = laser-guided bomb.

Before Operation Desert Storm, the USAF maintained almost 50,000 short tons of munitions in pre-positioned stocks. With a few minor exceptions—e.g., the RAF in Oman and the French in Djibouti—there are only a few small stockpiles in theater for allied forces.

Command and Control

For allied AEFs, command and control has at least two critical components: first, battle coordination, or the ability to synchronize the efforts of all the national contingents, and second, battlespace management, or the ability to see into the battlespace, locate targets within it, and promptly engage those targets before they can escape. The United States has played major roles in both of these key areas. The USAF automated planning systems that generate the air tasking order (ATO) and support rapid mission planning, for example, have been crucial to battle coordination. Likewise, U.S. imagery, the Joint Surveillance Target Attack Radar System (JSTARS), Rivet Joint, Airborne Warning and Control System (AWACS), and other reconnaissance platforms have been central to battlespace management. The key question, therefore, is whether the European allies have the capacity to interface with U.S. command-and-control systems. The answer is central to appreciating the overall effectiveness of allied air operations.

Currently, battle coordination presents major challenges to the Europeans. Although some allies—especially the French, Italians, and British—have had extended exposure to U.S. planning and ATOs, NATO has yet to adopt a uniform and complete set of battle coordination planning practices and tools. Interim tools, such as Power Scene, have emerged only recently as a result of operational demands in the Balkans. Future AEFs formed from "coalitions of the willing" may include some national contingents that still rely heavily on manual planning techniques. Whatever nations ultimately provide AEFs, battle coordination with current capabilities will require that the United States and its allies accommodate manual and automated planning to provide an ATO for all the contingents in a form they can use as well as to devise work-arounds for circumstances in which U.S. forces are not part of the deployment package.

The Europeans fare better in battlespace management. Although they lack Rivet Joint completely, some allies do have JSTARS–like aircraft that allow them to track some moving targets (e.g., the British Nimrod Star Window variant). The allies also have reasonable numbers of AEW aircraft as well as command-and-control aircraft such as the French E3F-SDCA, which, taken together, allow them to manage the battlespace. All of the key allies can also deploy good reconnaissance aircraft, and some supplement their fixed-wing aircraft with heliborne systems such as the French Horizon battlefield surveillance system. Several allies currently have first-generation UAVs as well. In addition, NATO infrastructure provides a limited number of AWACS platforms.

The Current Assessment

Under today's circumstances, the Europeans can certainly field enough fighter-bombers and support aircraft for two viable AEFs. However, their stocks of PGMs and lack of pre-positioned stockpiles in the region leave the Europeans inadequately prepared for the full range of possible enemy forces. RAND modeling indicates that against a six-division enemy force, the AEF had to fly some 1500 sorties and expend 6500 smart munitions to halt the enemy advance.[28] Of the munitions expended, just over 1700 of them would be European. Based on the evidence available, it is doubtful that the European allies possess enough guided bombs and missiles or in-theater stocks of other ordnance that might be used in lieu of the preferred weapons. If key allies—notably Britain, France, and Germany—were committed to the operation, allied inventories might be adequate against attacks of up to six divisions. Against nine to twelve division assaults, however—or under circumstances in which the better-armed allies do not play major roles—the European arsenal is likely to prove inadequate. (In 1990, Iraq attacked Kuwait with 11 divisions.)

Long-range deployment, contingent on the availability of suitable bases in the region, will not in all likelihood be constrained by a lack of transport and support aircraft to support the routine needs of the AEFs contemplated here. Leases and "market" arrangements seem more than adequate, since they were originally intended to deploy far more numerous ground forces and equipment. However, there is no amount of airlift that the Europeans are willing to procure that would compensate for Europe's lack of pre-positioned munitions stocks. Moreover, forward basing and force protection will probably be difficult if fully modern bases are not available or if the European forces are based within range of WMD. Under these circumstances, the lack of STO systems would leave European units vulnerable. The prospects of militarily effective operations are likewise uncertain. The lack of large quantities of precision munitions certainly undermines the probability that the allied forces could halt enemy seizure of critical energy installations. The chances of success are further

---

[28]The case in question is based on regular (as opposed to rapid) deployment of four U.S. and two European AEFs.

diminished by the questions that surround European battle coordination capabilities. In short, without the United States to cover their gaps, it is doubtful that European AEFs, with today's munitions and command-and-control arrangements, could make a significant contribution during the halt phase of a Persian Gulf MTW. But what of the future? The next section examines key allies' plans and the prospects for addressing present shortfalls.

FUTURE CAPABILITIES

The European allies have been taking steps to modernize their forces since the early 1990s, and most have undertaken comprehensive defense reviews or are now in the process of doing so. Recently, however, the long-term viability of these plans was called into question in a U.S. General Accounting Office report.[29] This report indicated that allied defense budgets may shrink in coming years to finance domestic programs and deficit reductions. Indeed, nowhere are these pressures more acute than in Germany, where defense budgets are projected to shrink from deutsche mark (DM) 47.1 billion this year to DM 43.7 billion in 2003.[30] France, too, has been forced to renege on earlier pledges to hold the line on its defense spending. Therefore, the possibility exists that the defense plans summarized below could be cut back.

United Kingdom

The future of the RAF was outlined in the British SDR.[31] In it, the British government committed to acquiring 232 Eurofighters to replace aging Tornado F3 and Jaguars. However, the plan called for an

---

[29]See U.S. General Accounting Office, *NATO: Implications of European Integration for Allies' Defense Spending*, GAO Report NSIAD-99-185, Washington, D.C., June 1999.

[30]For a comprehensive discussion of these budget pressures, see "European NATO Members Face Defense Budget Crunch, GAO Says," *Aerospace Daily*, July 30, 1999; "Country Briefing—Germany: Fighters to Eat Up Most of the Budget," *Jane's Defence Weekly*, Vol. 32, No. 1, July 7, 1999; and "Scharping hat kein Geld mehr für neue Transportflugzeuge," *Frankfurter Allgemeine Zeitung*, June 26, 1999.

[31]See http://www.mod.uk/policy/sdr/index.htm for the Web site devoted to the defense review. The formal presentation of the review to Parliament took place in July 1998.

overall reduction in attack/strike aircraft from 177 to 154 and for the reduction of air defense fighters from 100 to 87. The RAF will continue procurement plans for Brimstone and Stormshadow air-to-surface missiles, upgrade some Tornado GR4 aircraft, and improve the NBC and STO capabilities of the RAF Regiment. The SDR also made a commitment to continue seeking a replacement for the Tornado ground attack fleet. The place holder is known as the "Future Offensive Air System," and its requirements may be satisfied through the purchase of the Joint Strike Fighter or through the pursuit of other aircraft options.[32]

The RAF will undertake other improvements as well. Current ground attack aircraft, for example, are being outfitted with thermal imaging and laser designating pods to allow them to deliver Paveway II and III laser-guided bombs. Some 142 of these aircraft are also getting Global Positioning System (GPS) navigation systems and digital mapping systems. The Star Window variant of the Nimrod has been upgraded as well, and a follow-on airborne standoff radar (ASTOR) aircraft is expected to enter service in 2002. Britain has also been vigorously exploring precision munition options, including U.S., French, and German systems. A new advanced air-launched anti-armor weapon, for example, will replace the BL-755 cluster bomb throughout the RAF inventory. The RAF expects the new weapon to enter its arsenal beginning in 2000.[33]

France

France's armed forces are in the midst of a major strategic realignment and redirection that is scheduled to conclude in 2015. For the air force, the program has meant modernization for some current aircraft as well as acquisition of new aircraft and munitions. The fighter/attack aircraft inventory has grown with the delivery of 139 Rafale B fighters, and another 95 are on order. If all goes according to plan, the first wing of Rafale aircraft will be operational by 2002, with all the aircraft delivered by 2012. An electronic reconnaissance and observation version of Rafale is also on order. The air force is, more-

---

[32]*Strategic Defence Review*, "Future Military Capabilities," Supporting Essay Six, paragraphs 37–40, http://www.mod.uk/policy/sdr/essay06.htm.

[33]*USNI Periscope Database*, September 7, 1997.

over, in the process of taking delivery on Mirage 2000D strike aircraft, and older Mirage 2000 models are scheduled to be upgraded. France is also improving its air-to-air refueling capabilities with the installation of underwing flight refueling pods on 11 of its KC-135FR tankers.[34]

Precision attack will benefit from the delivery of new cruise and air-to-surface missiles. The Scalp variant of the Apache EG is slated for delivery beginning in 2003, and 500 of these cruise missiles have been ordered.   Other versions, including the shorter-range antirunway and area interdiction models, are being delivered now, with the order complete in 2002. Some 500 of these missiles should ultimately fill the French Air Force's arsenal. The Vesta air-to-surface missile is currently under development as well and is expected to be ready for delivery beginning in 2005. Five thousand direct attack weapons are in production as replacements for AS-30 laser-guided weapons and the Arcole laser-guided bomb; delivery is scheduled to begin in 2002.[35]

Less progress is evident in air defense and STO capabilities. France withdrew from the Medium Extended Air Defense System (MEADS), which Paris had agreed to pursue in cooperation with the United States, Italy, and Germany. No major acquisitions of collective NBC protection or other STO technologies have been announced.

Germany

The principal elements in future German Air Force programs are evident from an earlier study that established a framework for future German military planning. The air force will emphasize the integration of surveillance, command-and-control, and weapons systems. More specifically, it will pursue stealth and high-speed, high-capacity data processing to maintain and improve interoperability with U.S. forces.[36]

---

[34]*USNI Periscope Database*, February 1, 1999.

[35]Ibid.

[36]"Armed Forces Employment 2020," Federal German Ministry of Defense, Armed Forces Staff VI/2, September 30, 1996, pp. 51–55.

However ambitious the long-term plan for the air force may be, the near-term prospects are much more modest, emphasizing upgrades to current aircraft and systems. The Tornado strike/attack air fleet is undergoing modernization, which includes the ability to deliver AGM-65 Maverick and AGM-88 High-Speed Antiradiation Missiles (HARMs). The Tornadoes are also being outfitted with a new laser-designating pod that will allow for the use of the BLU-109 laser-guided bomb. The transport fleet of C-160 Transalls has undergone extensive refitting to extend their lives out to 2010, but budget pressures have clouded their replacement plans in uncertainty. Plans to buy two additional A310 transports fell victim to budget pressures and have been canceled. Germany is buying the Eurofighter and ultimately plans on 180 of these aircraft. Forty will be ground attack fighters and should begin entry into service in 2004.[37]

Munitions plans include the purchase of 400 BLU-109 laser-guided bombs. Germany is also developing the Taurus KEPD 350 air-to-surface missile in point attack, antirunway, cluster, antiarmor, and hard-target configurations. Initial operational capability should be around 2001. The air force will also receive ARAMIS, a replacement for the AGM-88 HARM. The new missile is expected to have a range of 100 km.[38]

Germany continues its modest participation in MEADS, which is scheduled to become operational in 2005. The air force has also signed an agreement with Lockheed Martin Vought to develop a German Patriot PAC-3 system as an interim, stopgap measure until MEADS is operational. Otherwise, there are no official indications of major work on force protection or STO capabilities.[39]

The aforementioned budget pressures could take their toll on Germany's military plans. For instance, Germany might terminate its role in MEADS and defer decisions about replacing the C-160 fleet. In addition, notwithstanding the central role the Eurofighter will play in the future German Air Force, Berlin may be forced to stretch the program to distribute the costs more evenly over a longer

---

[37] *USNI Periscope Database*, February 1, 1999.

[38] Ibid.

[39] Ibid. See also "Country Briefing—Germany."

period. As an extreme option, the Ministry of Defense may have to face the prospect of purchasing fewer aircraft. Finally, all the munitions programs would probably face reductions in their size and delays in their introduction into the force. In sum, defense spending cuts of the magnitude being contemplated by Berlin would hamper efforts to improve the power projection capabilities of the German armed forces.

Italy

Italy's New Defense Model plan has led to downsizing within the air force and intense pressures on overall defense spending. The current defense plan and cost overruns associated with acquisition of the Eurofighter have together created severe constraints on force modernization. Long-standing plans to purchase AEW aircraft have been shelved, although the Ministry of Defense has retained a requirement for four aircraft. Budget considerations have likewise foreclosed the opportunity to buy ECR Tornado aircraft and have forced the air force to lease 24 Tornado F3 air defense fighters from the U.K. Acquisition of precision munitions has slowed to a trickle.[40]

The Italian Air Force is, however, still in the process of buying Eurofighters. The service also remains involved in MEADS, which will improve its ability to defend its units deployed in a forward theater. The air force will eventually buy up to 44 Future Large Aircraft (FLA) and has recently purchased 18 U.S.-built C-130J transports. Current plans also call for the air force to launch a military communications satellite, Sicral, later this year. The satellite will handle UHF, VHF, and EHF traffic and will be protected against jamming. The air force expects it to support expeditionary operations.[41]

Netherlands

Most of the Netherlands' modernization program has been accomplished. As part of this effort, the air force upgraded much of its air fleet. Midlife upgrades are currently ongoing for the F-16 fleet and

---

[40]*USNI Periscope Database*, February 1, 1999.
[41]Ibid.

focus on improved electronic countermeasures (ECMs), better radar, and a modular mission computer. Sixty aircraft have been fitted with night navigation systems. Some of these aircraft are also getting laser designation pods to support Dutch Paveway II laser-guided bombs. Longer-term plans include acquisition of the U.S. Joint Strike Fighter as a replacement for the F-16 after 2010. The air force also plans to buy AGM-65G Mavericks and the AGM-154 Joint Stand-Off Weapon (JSOW), probably after 2000.[42]

Spain

Spain modernized its air forces in the mid-1990s, during which time the EF-18, Mirage F-1, RF-4C, and C-130 aircraft all received upgrades. In addition, Spain eventually plans to buy 87 Eurofighters. Madrid's munitions plans are modest and focus on purchasing new air-to-air missiles, leaving them with only marginal capability against ground forces.[43]

ASSESSING THE ADEQUACY OF CURRENT PLANS

Chapter Two postulated Iraqi armored assaults ranging in size from three to twelve divisions. This chapter began with the premise that in order to be effective in stopping an Iraqi invasion force, the allies would have to perform four key tasks: (1) get to the theater of operations, (2) establish bases from which to strike, (3) sustain and protect the forward-deployed units, and (4) carry out effective strikes. The key question, therefore, is: Given the allies' plans for future force development, how would they fare against an Iraqi invasion of Kuwait? Each of the key tasks is considered below.

All allied air forces can self-deploy, and there are enough tankers in the NATO nations' inventories to support the deployment of the aircraft associated with two European AEFs. The tankers will, however, need forward bases from which to fly. It is therefore important that Turkey and other allies make their air fields available to support the deployment of European AEFs. More important, the allies face seri-

---

[42] *USNI Periscope Database,* January 1, 1999.

[43] Ibid.

ous shortfalls in their capability to move the support package for AEFs both promptly and efficiently.

Virtually all of the allies remain dependent on fully developed airfields, although France and the U.K. have created limited capabilities to operate under austere conditions. If the allies were required to operate from more austere facilities, the requirements for supporting aircraft would escalate. In some instances, local contractors could be hired to provide services; in other cases, living quarters, latrine facilities, field kitchens, and a host of other support elements would have to be flown in. More important, rudimentary airstrips typically lack the ramp space, maintenance areas, and other flight operations support essential to sustaining high sortie rates.

A critical sustainment issue is whether the precision munitions available will be adequate for the job. Five of the six key allies plan to make major purchases of precision munitions. Of the acquisition initiatives reported in Table 4.6, the average of all 15 transactions was 512 weapons. If all six key allies make future purchases of 500 weapons each, the combined inventory would be 3000 through 2007. The range of precision munitions expended by the Europeans against a six-division Iraqi force modeled in other RAND work ran from about 1700 to 3200 munitions, depending on the details of each excursion. This suggests that the six-division case is near the upper limit of what the Europeans could sustain under this program. Unless they decided to buy larger stockpiles of these munitions than their recent practices and current plans call for, the Europeans would thus be likely to run out of PGMs in the most demanding circumstances surrounding a six-division-or-larger attacking force. In any event, these countries would not agree to use a 15-year accumulation of PGMs in a single operation. The absence of pre-positioned stocks in the theater further undermines Europe's potential contribution.

Force protection is a growing concern for all the allies. Despite efforts on the part of the RAF to improve its NBC protection, and despite plans for advanced Patriot PAC-3 and MEADS air defense systems, the vulnerability of allied air forces both to missiles and to NBC weapons is growing.[44] The modest steps being taken by the allies

---

[44]Peters and Deshong, *Out of Area or Out of Reach?*, Chapter 3.

may, moreover, be outstripped by the pace at which these weapons are proliferating. Among the allies, Spain is probably most vulnerable in this regard; Spanish forces have long lagged behind the other allies in NBC protection. No matter which ally is most or least prepared, however, none is fully prepared with a full suite of STO capabilities. A successful attack that produced mass casualties might lead some allies to withdraw from the operation.

Some of the allies' plans will certainly make them more effective in halt-phase operations. Five of the six key allies, for example, will have better ECM pods for their attack aircraft, and all will have at least some aircraft with laser designating pods. Most will also have modern PGMs, including advanced antiradiation missiles. There is little doubt, therefore, that future allied AEFs will be better equipped both to fly against very demanding targets and to destroy those targets.

At the same time, the suitability of the allies' battle command and battlespace management capabilities is more questionable. Plans for Star Window, Atlantique 2 Plus, and similar aircraft will help the allies see the battlespace in greater depth and detail. The cooperation and experience that comes from NATO operations like Allied Force is also important. However, current allied plans do not show evidence of shared or interoperable automated mission-planning and command-and-control systems that are capable of moving high volumes of data. The ability to generate effective strikes thus remains limited by the allies' uneven capacity for processing and responding to an ATO. In sum, only by undertaking improvements in missile defense, command-and-control capability, and munitions stockpiles can the European allies develop an effective air-to-ground capability against armored forces. The preceding discussion and RAND modeling suggest that if the Europeans made those improvements, they could play a significant role in the halt phase in combination with U.S. air forces; indeed, if the U.S. military were heavily engaged elsewhere, the contribution of one to two European AEFs might well prove critical.

ALLIED CONTRIBUTIONS OF NICHE CAPABILITIES

America's European allies confront two major challenges: adapting their forces to out-of-area operations and managing the technological gap with the United States. At a minimum, declines in allied defense spending will need to be stopped and defense spending priorities altered. In some areas, moreover, these changes will not come cheaply or easily. European defense spending may need to increase at a time when allied governments face strong pressure to cut defense expenditures. According to one NATO official, "It would take the Europeans two decades to catch up with the Americans (technologically) even if they had the money and the will to spend it."[45] Under these circumstances, European governments will have to shift investment priorities and make tradeoffs, and there will be a strong temptation to sacrifice the "niche" capabilities described below to fund other priorities—assets that could prove useful in a variety of Gulf military contingencies that threaten common Western security interests.

Access and Basing

Across the range of out-of-area contingencies, the most critical allied support will often be in the form of access and basing privileges. Notwithstanding the successful use of the B-2 bombers flying from the continental United States (CONUS) in Operation Allied Force, the USAF will continue to rely on in-theater bases for beddown of shorter-range combat assets.

European partners are also pivotal in supporting mobility operations as well as in providing overflight, transit, basing, fuel, and crew rest stops for strategic airlifters and operating bases for intratheater transports. Support aircraft such as tankers, AWACS, JSTARS, and U-2 aircraft also rely on beddown locations in allied countries.

As the USAF evolves into an "expeditionary aerospace force," it will require new logistics concepts to facilitate its engagement and power projection activities. Whether called "regional contingency cen-

---

[45]See William Drozdiak, "War Showed U.S.-Allied Inequality," *Washington Post,* June 28, 1999.

ters,"[46] or "forward support locations,"[47] one powerful concept is to establish a small number of large, well-stocked operating bases in secure locations around the world. Using these facilities as "hubs," support could flexibly swing across regions, servicing bases from which operations are being executed. Given their long history of political and military cooperation, shared interests in energy security and other issues, and a wealth of well-developed infrastructure, NATO partners would clearly be good candidates to play host to this kind of installation.

Tactical Reconnaissance and Electronic Warfare

Since the retirement of the RF-4E, F-4G, and EF-111, the U.S. Air Force no longer operates dedicated tactical reconnaissance and electronic warfare aircraft. While some of those capabilities are provided by other platforms—e.g., by UAVs such as the Predator, Navy and Marine Corps EA-6B jamming aircraft, and F-16s equipped to perform a version of the "Wild Weasel" surface-to-air-missile (SAM) hunting mission—the experience in Operation Allied Force demonstrated that these assets are in short supply.[48] As the threat evolves—with Iran or Iraq potentially possessing more sophisticated SAMs such as the SA-10 or SA-12 as well as more dangerous mobile SAMs such as the SA-11—any existing shortfalls, particularly in electronic warfare, are likely to be exacerbated.

Several allied aircraft could help fill this gap. Both the German and Italian air forces fly the ECR version of the Tornado twin-engine fighter-bomber. The Tornado ECR is equipped with a precision locator system for detecting and locating hostile emitters and is armed with HARM missiles for antiradar attack. It also has a

---

[46]U.S. Air Force Scientific Advisory Board, *Report on United States Air Force Expeditionary Forces, Volume 1: Summary*, Washington, D.C., 1997.

[47]P. Killingsworth et al., *Flexbasing: Achieving Global Presence for Expeditionary Aerospace Forces*, RAND, MR-1113-AF, 2000.

[48]For example, the USAF reports losing four Predators in Operation Allied Force, and the loss of an F-117 aircraft early in the Kosovo campaign has been attributed in part to the absence of jamming support at a key point in the mission. See Peter Skibitski, "Pentagon to Create Additional EA-6B Prowler Unit to Meet Demands," *Inside the Navy*, August 30, 1999, and David A. Fulghum, "Kosovo Report to Boost New JSF Jamming Role," *Aviation Week and Space Technology*, August 30, 1999.

forward-looking infrared sensor and an infrared line scanner for passive reconnaissance. The British RAF operates reconnaissance variants of both the Tornado and the Jaguar. Both were employed extensively in Operation Allied Force.

Other NATO air forces operate tactical reconnaissance aircraft as well. Some Dutch, Danish, and Belgian F-16s have been modified to carry reconnaissance pods, while Poland flies the MiG-21R reconnaissance aircraft and the Czech Republic operates a small number of Su-22 FITTERs in the reconnaissance role. Finally, the French air force is equipped with 40 Mirage F-1CR reconnaissance aircraft.

Airborne Early Warning

Boeing E-3 AWACS aircraft are among the USAF's most important, and most overtaxed, assets. A vital "force multiplier," AWACS planes and crews have been called upon to perform almost nonstop deployments—monitoring no-fly zones, supporting strike operations, and the like—since the end of the Cold War. Thus, managing the wear and tear on the USAF's fleet of 33 E-3 aircraft and the men and women who fly them constitutes one of the most serious operational challenges facing the Air Force today.

 Fortunately, NATO is in a position to help. The Alliance itself operates 18 AWACS aircraft as the NATO Airborne Early Warning (NAEW) forces. France has taken delivery of four E-3F models, and the U.K. flies seven E-3Ds. Together, these aircraft roughly equal the USAF inventory and could contribute significantly to any NATO out-of-area operation in the greater Middle East or elsewhere.[49]

---

[49]There are a number of technical differences between the various models; the British and French aircraft, for example, have engines that differ from those of the U.S. and NATO planes. All, however, are capable of performing the basic functions of AEW and intercept control. All USAF, U.K., and NATO aircraft are also undergoing a radar system improvement program (RSIP) to increase the ability of the AWACS to detect small and/or stealthy targets, to improve its electronic counter-countermeasure performance, and to enhance its maintainability.

Theater Airlift

No NATO country other than the United States currently operates a strategic airlift fleet of any consequence, although Great Britain's recent SDR called for the acquisition of six C-17-equivalent aircraft.[50] As Figure 4.2 shows, however, no fewer than 11 non-U.S. NATO members fly the C-130 Hercules medium transport. Germany, France, and Turkey fly the Franco-German C-160 Transall, a twin-engine transport of similar performance to the C-130. Thus, the Netherlands is the only militarily active NATO member of more than a year's standing that operates no airlifter in the C-130 class.

Together, non-U.S. NATO air forces operate more than 150 of various C-130 models along with 114 C-160s, and Italy flies 36 G-222 medium

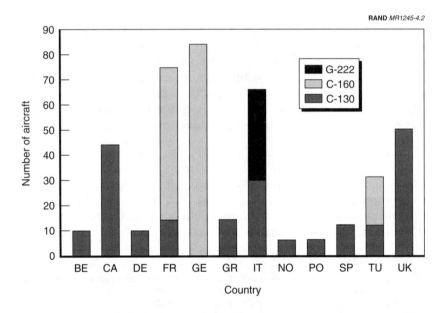

Figure 4.2—Theater Airlifters Operated by Non-U.S. NATO Members

---

[50]The FLA is supposed to be the first European strategic airlifter since the 1950s. Although the program is proceeding, escalating cost estimates and the possible defection of several key partners, including Germany and Britain, have placed its future in doubt.

transports. America's European partners together have about 300 theater airlifters in their inventories; this compares favorably to the 201 C-130s in the active USAF force structure and constitutes more than half of the 540 Hercules operated by the total air force.

Special Relationships and Special Forces

Many of America's NATO allies have relationships with key countries in the greater Middle East that stretch back to colonial days. Great Britain, for example, put the Hashemites on the Jordanian throne. France and Belgium, meanwhile, retain fairly close contact with various nations in Central Africa as well as in Syria and Lebanon, while Paris, Madrid, and Rome have interests in and close ties to the governments of North Africa. Because of these historical ties and cultural affinities, some Middle Eastern regimes might find it more palatable to deal with non-U.S. NATO governments under some circumstances. This political leverage could prove valuable in negotiations for access or overflight rights or in attempts to navigate the treacherous terrain in the intranational conflicts depicted in some of the scenarios described in Chapter Two.

These bonds of history may also make some allied special forces particularly useful in the region. The British Special Air Service (SAS), for example, was essentially born in the desert. Created to operate behind German lines in North Africa during World War II, the SAS has evolved from a force dedicated to harassing Rommel's rear area to one of the most respected special forces organizations in the world.

French special forces are about 1000 strong. In addition, the 8500-man Foreign Legion serves as an elite force for overseas use, with one regiment stationed in Djibouti. The Spanish Legion Extranjera has similar capabilities and is partially dedicated to the rapid reaction mission. A number of other NATO countries maintain small special forces establishments that could be valuable for missions such as intelligence collection, training of indigenous troops, direct action, and support of allied air operations.

Countermine Warfare

Sea mining constitutes a considerable threat in the Strait of Hormuz and in the Persian Gulf. During the 1991 Gulf War, two U.S. warships—the Aegis cruiser USS *Princeton* and the amphibious assault ship USS *Tripoli*—struck Iraqi mines; according to some reports, the *Princeton* was nearly lost while the *Tripoli* suffered a 16- by 20-foot hole 10 feet beneath her waterline. The narrow Strait, meanwhile, seems an ideal place for offensive mine warfare, and many scenarios for Iranian aggression in the Gulf prominently feature maritime mine warfare. Countering these weapons could thus play an important role in any conflict in the Gulf.

Defeating naval mines is a complex, time-consuming, and resource-intensive process. Throughout the Cold War, the U.S. Navy focused on open-ocean, "blue water" operations, placing little emphasis on countermine warfare.[51] Despite its commitment to littoral operations, the U.S. Navy still fields relatively modest mine warfare assets; only 15 mine warfare ships are in the active navy, with 13 more to be found in the Naval Reserve Fleet.[52] Unlike major naval combatants, these vessels are not self-deploying over long distances; with fairly limited endurance and top speeds in the 10- to 14-knot range, they are typically transported to the area of interest on super-heavy-lift cargo ships. This is how, for example, the USS *Avenger* and three other U.S. mine countermeasure ships deployed to the Persian Gulf in 1990 during Operation Desert Shield.[53]

Other NATO countries, particularly those with a North Sea or Baltic orientation, have paid more attention and devoted more resources to the problems of mine warfare. The Danish navy, for example, has 14 mine warfare vessels on its rolls, with 14 more modern mine countermeasure (MCM) ships on order. The French, Belgians, and Dutch

---

[51] Indeed, 25 years elapsed between the completion of the last large ocean-going minesweeper for the U.S. Navy, the *Assurance* in 1958, and the laying down of the first Avenger class in 1983.

[52] One of these ships, the USS *Inchon*, was converted from an amphibious assault ship into a mine operations command vessel. Although it can carry up to eight mine warfare helicopters, it has no intrinsic countermine capabilities.

[53] Today the U.S. Navy maintains two mine countermeasure ships, the USS *Ardent* and the USS *Dextrous*, on station in the Gulf area and rotates crews for them.

cooperated in designing and building the "Tripartie" mine warfare ship in the 1980s and 1990s. All 35 vessels are undergoing extensive modernization, and several Dutch ships will also be fitted as command platforms for the "Troika" deep-water mine-sweeping drones (which are also fielded by Germany).[54] In addition to its seven "Tripartie" vessels, Belgium is also procuring four new MCMs and has two mine warfare command-and-support ships.

Britain's Royal Navy sails 21 modern mine warfare ships and is constructing five more new Sandown-class MCMs, four of which will also be built by Spain. Italy deploys a dozen new mine warfare vessels; in fact, its *Lerici* design was the basis for the U.S. Navy's new Osprey-class mine hunters (MCH). Germany has 12 1990s-vintage Frankenthal–class MCHs among its fleet of 32 mine warfare vessels.

Canada built 12 Kingston-class mine hunters between 1995 and 1999; although the ships are being employed as multipurpose coastal-defense vessels, they retain all their design countermine capability. The Norwegian navy has 12 advanced double-hulled surface-effect mine hunters and minesweepers of the Oksoy and Alta classes.

Chemical Warfare

The capability of NATO allies to operate in an environment contaminated by chemical agents is limited. However, some new Alliance members have competencies in this area dating from their Warsaw Pact days that equal or exceed those of the U.S. armed forces. For example, when the U.S. Army urgently needed an NBC reconnaissance capability during the run-up to the Gulf War, it acquired a variant of the former East German TPZ-1 Fuchs ("Fox") wheeled armored personnel carrier (APC); eventually about 120 were purchased (designated the M93 in U.S. service).

The former Warsaw Pact countries were also regarded as having taken the prospect of NBC warfare fairly seriously. As a result, their militaries possess credible NBC reconnaissance and decontamina-

---

[54]There are 15 Alkmaar class in the Netherlands service, 13 Eridan class in the French navy, and seven Aster class in Belgium. Greece also has three Tripartie-class ships acquired from the Netherlands.

tion capabilities. The Czech and Hungarian armies, for example, operate NBC reconnaissance variants of the OT-65 and BTR-80 APCs,
respectively, while Poland employs a version of the BRDM-2 for the
same purpose.

Chapter Five

IMPLICATIONS AND RECOMMENDATIONS FOR THE USAF AND U.S. DEFENSE PLANNING

Richard Sokolsky, F. Stephen Larrabee, and Stuart Johnson

This study has addressed several questions that are central to the future of defense planning for the United States and its NATO allies: What are the most serious threats to Persian Gulf security and other Western energy resources over the next ten to fifteen years? Under what conditions can the United States rely on allied military contributions to defend these resources? What types of military contributions does the United States need from its European allies? If the United States needs allied military contributions to protect oil supplies, what force improvements should Washington press allies to make to upgrade their capabilities for power projection? What changes, if any, should the USAF make in its doctrine, training, organization, plans, operations, and procurement to capitalize fully on allied contributions?

THREATS TO WESTERN ENERGY SECURITY

This study has reaffirmed the fact that, given its geopolitical significance and its dominant role in the global energy market, only the Persian Gulf warrants planning for U.S.-led coalition operations to ensure Western access to critical energy supplies.

It is highly unlikely that the United States would commit combat forces to maintain the flow of Caspian or North African energy supplies. These regions make only a paltry contribution to global energy security, and, in the case of the Caspian, Western military intervention is unlikely because of the danger of a Russian military response. A prolonged cutoff of North African natural gas exports would have more serious political and economic consequences for southern NATO members (e.g., Spain, Italy, France); if this were to happen, these countries might assemble a European-led force to restore access. In this context, the United States might agree to requests for assistance (e.g., logistics and intelligence support), but a U.S. commitment of combat forces would be unlikely. Likewise, although the United States might provide assistance to Turkish forces if Ankara chose to defend Turkish access to Caspian oil and gas resources, the United States would be unlikely to provide combat forces. In short, when it comes to the use of U.S. combat forces to protect energy supplies, only the Persian Gulf merits the attention of U.S. force planning.

Planning for an MTW in the Persian Gulf will therefore remain a focus of U.S. defense planning for the foreseeable future even if the U.S. two-MTW strategy is modified. Both Iran and Iraq harbor aspirations for regional hegemony, while the United States seeks to preserve its predominant position in the Gulf. Moreover, the United States and these countries have fundamentally different visions of a security structure for the Gulf. U.S. policy is aimed at containing Iraq's and Iran's expansionist ambitions through a combination of sanctions, security arrangements, and military presence. The current regimes in Baghdad and Tehran, on the other hand, seek to eliminate U.S. influence and military presence in the Gulf as well as to establish their domination not only over the Gulf states but also, more specifically, over oil production and pricing decisions. And in the future they may well brandish WMD and terrorist threats to further their aims.

Thus, until Iraq and Iran become responsible members of the international community, U.S. preparations to defeat large-scale aggression will be essential to sustaining deterrence, demonstrating U.S. security commitment to the Gulf states, and maintaining American predominance in a region that is vital to Western security. Moreover, it is highly likely that the United States would use force to fulfill its security commitments in the Gulf if such preparations failed to deter aggression.

At the same time, however, the prospect of large-scale Iraqi or Iranian military attacks against the Gulf Arab states is remote for at least the next five to ten years. Iraqi and Iranian conventional capabilities have been decimated by war, sanctions, and a lack of resources to spend on defense. The long-term prospect of lower oil prices, coupled with the need to fund massive economic reconstruction, will make it difficult if not impossible to fund a sustained force modernization program. Perhaps more important, the Baghdad and Tehran regimes are likely to be increasingly preoccupied with their own survival over the coming years. They almost certainly calculate that they would suffer a major defeat in a confrontation with the United States, which would trigger widespread discontent and perhaps threaten their hold on power.

In the short to medium term, therefore, Iraq and perhaps to a lesser extent Iran are likely to use other means to challenge the geopolitical status quo in the Gulf and U.S. domination of the region. The two most likely options are (1) WMD, terrorism, and subversion, and (2) limited air and missile attacks or small-scale ground incursions aimed at seizing limited territory or assets. The aim of these "salami" tactics will be to probe for soft spots, test the limits of U.S. resolve, and intimidate the Gulf states without provoking a massive U.S. military response.

In sum, in contradistinction to the scenarios that tend to dominate U.S. force planning, Iraqi and Iranian nonconventional warfare represents the most plausible threats to Western security interests in the Gulf. Accordingly, the United States and its European allies must be prepared to deal not only with the "canonical" MTW threat but also with a broader spectrum of more plausible Iraqi and Iranian challenges. The ambiguous and indirect nature of these challenges will complicate U.S. efforts to reach a consensus with its European partners on the appropriate response to limited Iraqi and Iranian provocations.

THE ALLIED CONTRIBUTION TO ENERGY SECURITY

Under what circumstances could allied military contributions make a difference in protecting Western access to vital energy supplies? Are America's European allies capable of providing such a contribution? As suggested in this study, the perception of a good part of the

U.S. military that the United States does not "need" the help of its European allies in the Gulf requires some qualification. The results of recent RAND research highlight two major conclusions. First, if the USAF promptly deploys a large force (four AEFs or more) to a Gulf contingency, allied air contributions would be of marginal importance. Second, if the USAF is engaged in an MTW elsewhere and the Gulf is the "second MTW," a prompt allied deployment of one to three AEFs could in fact prove critical in halting an Iraqi armored invasion.

The prospects that America's European partners will develop the capability to deploy three AEFs is unlikely, though one or perhaps two AEFs may indeed be feasible. As John Peters, David Shlapak, and Timothy Liston note in Chapter Four, some allies—notably the U.K. and France—are making steady progress in developing the capability to transport large forces to the theater of operations. Possessing adequate strike platforms and transport-and-support aircraft for long-range deployment is not, however, enough to ensure effective combat operations. European countries face serious shortcomings in their current power projection capabilities. The most serious shortfalls are inadequate command and control, limited quantities of advanced precision munitions, and the vulnerability of Europe's forces to attack at forward bases. Together, these limitations raise serious questions about the military utility of European AEF operations in the Gulf.

It would be a mistake, moreover, to underestimate the dimensions of the problems the European allies will confront in rectifying these deficiencies and restructuring their forces to cope with shifting security priorities. NATO countries face difficult choices in their defense planning that have been complicated by the ESDP and by the emerging threat of ballistic missile attack by hostile states.

For most of its history, the United States has fought its major wars thousands of miles from its own shores; therefore, it has long been an "expeditionary" power that has devoted substantial resources to acquiring the wherewithal for power projection. By contrast, apart from limited colonial actions and the Falklands War of 1982, European militaries—especially since the early 1960s—have concentrated on fighting wars much closer to home. As such, they lack the political, psychological, and cultural mindset of expeditionary powers as well as the critical "enablers" for power projection. Acquiring these capabilities and catching up with U.S. high-tech capabilities will not come cheaply or easily.

Since 1990, defense spending among non-U.S. NATO allies has decreased by 25 percent as a percentage of gross domestic product (GDP).[1] Procurement and research and development (R&D) budgets, in particular, have been starved for funds. The United States spends roughly $35 billion annually on military R&D, while the rest of NATO spends only $9 billion. Although the U.S. defense budget as a share of GDP declined at a higher rate (35 percent) than those of its NATO allies during the early to mid-1990s, American spending remained much higher in absolute terms. For example, whereas the United States devotes about 3.2 percent of its GNP to defense, Germany allocates only 1.5 percent of its GNP to defense and has announced that it will cut defense spending by $10 billion over the next four years. Thus, while some new U.S. programs were canceled and others were either slowed or scaled back, U.S. modernization has proceeded and new capabilities have continued to enter the U.S. force at a relatively rapid rate.

As a result, the United States and its NATO partners face serious interoperability challenges, with the Europeans lacking many of the advanced weapons, technologies, and techniques that U.S. forces possess. Whether in the area of precision munitions, advanced C^3 systems, logistics support, or intelligence collection, fusion, and distribution systems, considerable gaps have opened between U.S. and European capabilities. These gaps were manifested in Operation Allied Force, in which the United States provided 80 percent of usable air power and carried out the most challenging missions, such as precision strikes in overcast or marginal weather. Yet European militaries face an uphill battle in meeting the twin challenges of adapting and equipping for long-distance power projection and closing the technological gap with the United States.

European governments are therefore in the devilish predicament of asking their publics and parliaments to spend substantial economic resources on investments in military capabilities for contingencies

---

[1]See Department of Defense, *Report on Allied Contributions to the Common Defense,* Washington, D.C., March 1998.

that are both controversial and, in some cases, unlikely. Some observers argue that European governments would not have to increase defense spending significantly to improve power projection capabilities; instead, they maintain that such enhancements would require only that these governments spend scarce resources differently. According to this view, the problem is not that Europe lacks sufficient forces but rather that most European forces (Britain and France excepted) are currently configured to defend borders that are no longer seriously threatened. To close the current technological gap, these observers claim, European countries need to reduce the size of their ground forces, consolidate defense industries, and use the resulting dividends to develop improved power projection capabilities.

This point is well taken but needs to be put in a broader perspective. In the first instance, many of the capabilities and systems the United States is encouraging its allies to buy are expensive and would thus lie beyond the means of countries with small defense budgets even if investment priorities were shifted. Second and more important, reordering European budget and defense spending priorities, as in the United States, poses painful choices that most politicians in democratic countries prefer to avoid. This will be particularly true over the long term, when defense spending will face growing downward pressure as European governments attempt to grapple with the escalating costs of entitlement burdens.[2] Third, the introduction of doctrinal, operational, and force structure innovations into military organizations, which are inherently conservative, usually meets with stiff institutional and cultural resistance, as most such changes are seen as a threat to existing norms, habits, and procedures.

As many observers have noted, it is for precisely these reasons that, a decade after the Cold War, the United States essentially continues to maintain a smaller version of its Cold War force structure and has failed to undertake the kind of restructuring, reorganization, and renovation that is necessary to adapt the U.S. military establishment to new security threats and challenges. European governments and

---

[2]The U.S. General Accounting Office recently concluded that this budget environment will confront the European allies with significant challenges in sustaining defense modernization. See U.S. GAO, *NATO: Implications of European Integration for Allies' Defense Spending.*

militaries are not immune to pressures to stick to "business as usual." Those who believe that European militaries can reinvent themselves "on the cheap"—or without political and institutional pain—have ignored the American military's difficult transition to the post–Cold War security environment.

Apart from the question of capabilities, there is also the matter of political will. In all but an MTW that posed a serious threat to vital Western security interests, the United States will face difficulties in garnering widespread allied military participation in "coalitions of the willing" to defend the security of the Persian Gulf. As Richard Sokolsky, F. Stephen Larrabee, and Ian Lesser point out in Chapter Three, most European governments (except the U.K. and France) confront serious political and economic constraints on their ability to engage in combat outside Europe and to acquire the power projection capabilities necessary for such operations. Equally important, many also have different perspectives of threats, interests, and objectives:

- Most European governments do not share the U.S. assessment of the Iraqi and Iranian threat in general and harbor far less anxiety about the Iraqi and Iranian WMD threat in particular. Such governments are, for example, far less concerned about Iraq's and Iran's ability to reconstitute a credible force projection capability that would threaten their neighbors. On the whole, they are also less concerned about the Iraqi and Iranian ballistic missile threat to Europe.

- There is a fissure within the Alliance over the most effective means of thwarting the Iraqi and Iranian challenge. Broadly speaking, most European countries prefer strategies of engagement rather than confrontation as well as the use of "soft" rather than "hard" power to moderate Iranian and, to a lesser extent, Iraqi behavior.

- U.S. perceptions of Alliance interests do not always coincide with those of the European allies. In a crisis, many European governments may thus continue to diverge from U.S. views or express greater reluctance to use force. This is especially likely to be the case for smaller threats, such as military operations aimed at punishing misbehavior or influencing the outcome of internal power struggles.

- Allied governments face strong domestic pressure to reduce defense expenditures to free up funds for social programs while also confronting opposition to the use of force outside Europe. Kosovo underscored the difficulty of conducting such combat operations, especially for the Europeans, and the Gulf would present even greater impediments, both politically and militarily. In many allied countries, government support for military intervention in the Persian Gulf, especially in the absence of a U.N. mandate, is likely to prove divisive.

In sum, there is pervasive "Euro-skepticism" about extending the Alliance's security umbrella to the Persian Gulf. Thus, NATO is unlikely to define the Persian Gulf as an area of direct responsibility any time soon. Similarly, the United States can rely on only a small number of allies to commit combat forces in a "coalition of the willing" to military operations in the Gulf—and then only if these countries perceive a direct threat to vital national security interests and if Western military action has been endorsed by the UNSC. In the absence of these conditions, only the U.K. is likely to fight alongside the United States.

The United States thus finds itself in a paradoxical situation with respect to allied military contributions to Persian Gulf defense. In the most serious but implausible scenario—an Iraqi or Iranian MTW— several allies are indeed likely to join a "coalition of the willing." At the same time, however, broader allied participation is more problematic in the more likely event that the United States faces less serious contingencies such as limited military strikes, WMD attack, terrorism, and subversion.

CONCLUSIONS

Almost 25 years ago, the United States assumed a commitment to use force—unilaterally if necessary—to defend the Persian Gulf against outside attack. This security commitment has been reaffirmed by successive administrations and has been codified in U.S. operational planning. U.S. force planning for the Persian Gulf does not, however, assume allied military participation, and thus little effort has been made to develop the combined plans and capabilities that would be necessary to carry out effective coalition operations. A central question raised by this study is whether this planning assumption remains valid today and for the future and, if this is not the case, what adjustments need to be made.

Given the foregoing analysis as well as broader strategic and political considerations, we believe that the U.S. military needs to think in fresh ways about how best to utilize the military capabilities of allied countries for military operations in the Persian Gulf. The United States has the capability, acting alone, to halt a sizable Iraqi armored invasion of Kuwait and Saudi Arabia with little loss of territory as well as to repel Iraqi ground forces from occupied territory in a devastating counteroffensive. American forces, in particular, are highly adept at killing Iraqi tanks and other armored equipment with accurate, multiple-kill, air-delivered antiarmor munitions, even at night and in marginal weather. Therefore, it is by no means clear that asking America's European allies to duplicate these capabilities represents a cost-effective investment of limited resources unless the United States faces shortfalls that allied capabilities could redress or the allies could provide unique niche capabilities to complement U.S. forces—e.g., tactical reconnaissance and electronic warfare.[3]

The political and operational limits on European military contributions to combat operations outside Europe pose a dilemma for the United States as well as some difficult choices and tradeoffs. From a strictly war-fighting perspective, for example, the United States need not depend on allied military capabilities to achieve a decisive victory in the "canonical" Persian Gulf MTW as long as U.S. forces are not occupied with an MTW elsewhere and deploy promptly to the Gulf. To the contrary, unilateral military operations are easier to conduct than coalition operations in that they pose fewer problems with respect to C^3, logistics support, and harmonization of doctrine and tactics. Thus, unless the necessary planning and preparations have been undertaken in advance, multinational participation may actually reduce the effectiveness of military operations in the Gulf.

---

[3]The heavy burdens on the U.S. mobility forces and the adverse impact of cutbacks in USAF electronic warfare capabilities have been well documented. See Bryant Jordan, "Overloaded," *Air Force Times*, August 30, 1999, and David A. Fulghum, "Kosovo Conflict Spurred New Airborne Technology Use," *Aviation Week and Space Technology*, August 23, 1999.

That said, the United States would gain important political and strategic benefits from serious allied force contributions to Persian Gulf defense. The United States and Europe share common interests in Persian Gulf security even if the two may not always agree on the nature of the threats to those interests or on the most effective means of coping with such threats. Moreover, the United States is feeling the strain of meeting its security commitments in the Gulf as well as its other global military commitments. America's European partners, meanwhile, have the wealth, resources, and interests to play a more meaningful role in advancing common Western security objectives in the Gulf. More robust U.S.-European cooperation in safeguarding these interests would therefore reinvigorate a broader partnership whose vitality is essential to addressing the most serious challenges facing the United States and Europe today. In short, a Europe that is better able to project power into the Persian Gulf not only will be a better global partner for the United States but will also, as this study suggests, produce more security than the United States could achieve if it acted alone.

In addition, there are risks to the United States' bearing the burden of leadership in the Gulf alone. Sustaining the transatlantic relationship into the new millennium will require the support of European and American publics and legislatures that are increasingly focused inward—and that lack a shared vision of strategic purpose or a full appreciation of the benefits of a partnership that is more global, more equitable, and more ambitious.[4] The Euro-Atlantic relationship would be severely strained if a major threat to vital Western interests emerged in the Gulf and the United States were left virtually alone to counter it. The damage to these ties could, moreover, be incalculable if America suffered major combat losses. In short, U.S. global strategy is predicated on the assumption that the allies will engage in joint military actions to protect common interests. This strategy—as well as the U.S.-European partnership—would be dealt a serious blow if the European allies were perceived as shirking their responsibilities in a wider Persian Gulf war.

---

[4]For a fuller elaboration of this theme, see Gompert and Larrabee, *America and Europe*.

A key challenge, therefore, lies in reconciling military requirements with broader strategic and political imperatives. The United States must be realistic about European limitations and about the scope of the military contribution it can expect from its allies. Most European allies will be unable to overcome deep-seated constraints on extending Western military commitments beyond Europe and developing the power projection capabilities to make these commitments credible. Therefore, it would be highly imprudent for the U.S. military to forgo certain military capabilities or force modernization with the expectation that its allies will make up the difference.

Likewise, it makes little sense—politically, economically, or militarily—for the United States to urge sweeping, across-the-board improvements in allied power projection capabilities for military operations in the Gulf. It would be ill conceived, for instance, to press some of our European allies to spend scarce resources to replicate core U.S. capabilities at the expense of maintaining other "niche" capabilities that could prove useful in a wide range of Gulf contingencies (e.g., MCM capabilities, electronic warfare, and tactical reconnaissance). In other words, the United States should resist the impulse to clone a smaller, allied "lite" version of its Persian Gulf MTW force and the U.S. RMA force. In general, the United States does not need a European RMA force for the Gulf—but it does need compatible and complementary European capabilities.

These considerations reinforce the need for the United States and interested, like-minded allies to develop a comprehensive and integrated plan for coordinated force development and coalition operations. Such an effort would be designed to reach agreement on a division of labor that would encourage willing allies to do what they are good at while the United States concentrates on what it does best. In so doing, it would minimize the possibility of duplication and inefficient use of resources while exploiting the comparative advantage that individual allies bring to the table.

To suggest the need for this kind of undertaking is to underscore the need for wide-ranging innovations in NATO's defense planning process. The first step in implementing such an initiative would be to establish an appropriate planning mechanism. In this context, two options merit consideration. First, such planning could be carried out within an Alliance framework, taking advantage of NATO's CJTF concept and its existing headquarters and planning assets to plan and coordinate coalition operations among willing and able allies. Second, planning could be conducted outside Alliance channels, either in bilateral military-to-military discussions or in a multilateral format among key allies.[5]

These approaches are by no means mutually exclusive, and each has its strengths and weaknesses. Relying on NATO's institutional strengths and habits of cooperation, for example, would constitute the most efficient and effective use of planning resources but might be more than the traffic would bear. By contrast, bilateral talks would have the advantage of ease and simplicity and would be likely to produce quicker progress but would make the coordination of national and multinational plans more difficult. A multinational venue would facilitate coordinated development of power projection capabilities and combined plans for coalition operations. However, such a format, even if kept informal, could prove unwieldy and might slow progress. On balance, our preferred choice would be to build on the CJTF concept to develop a combined planning cell for coalition operations, supplemented as necessary by bilateral discussions. If such an approach encounters resistance within the Alliance, the establishment of a multilateral planning process outside NATO channels would be a suitable fallback, particularly since the Alliance as a whole is unlikely to engage in military operations beyond Europe.

The main purpose of this planning mechanism would be to formulate coordinated multinational plans for (1) the development of national power projection capabilities and (2) the conduct of coalition operations for the defense of critical energy supplies. In particular, the United States and its NATO allies would:

Advocate new force goals. The establishment of new force goals in allied defense planning is long overdue. Kosovo and the DCI highlight the need for specific capabilities, particular advanced PGMs, NBC protective capabilities, and STO systems. Thus, discussions of munitions force goals should carefully examine future requirements

---

[5]For a more detailed discussion of steps to improve European power projection capabilities and combined planning for coalition operations, see Peters and Deshong, *Out of Area or Out of Reach?*, pp. 126–127.

for precision munitions and pre-positioned stocks in or adjacent to critical theaters, including air-to-surface missiles, guided bombs, and antiradiation missiles. Since future operations are likely to be "coalitions of the willing," involving some but not all allies, these munitions talks should also embrace a range of issues. For example, they might consider the advantages of specialization among countries against the feasibility of creating complete strike packages so that any member might have a full range of offensive air capabilities from radar suppression to wide-area attack. The overriding objective of munitions force-goal development talks should be to ensure that the allies can sustain a protracted campaign that requires PGMs in substantial numbers.

Force goals for NBC should concentrate on identifying requirements for NBC protection for forward-based units. Goals should be negotiated for collective NBC shelters and medical facilities; improved individual protection, including vaccinations and pretreatments; and deployable aircraft decontamination equipment. The objective of the force goal talks should be to develop NBC protective capabilities across the Alliance that will make NBC-related risks manageable.

A new force goal should also be established for STO systems. The objective in negotiating this goal should be to create fully compatible air defense, theater missile defense, and air attack warning systems so that allied forces can operate within a safe area. These air and missile systems must also be integrated with NBC sensors and warning systems. The United States should lead the discussion and help the allies chart a course toward robust STO capabilities that will mature more quickly than the threat.

Reexamine Alliance infrastructure. The United States should explore with its allies the prospects for expanding NATO infrastructure to provide essential capabilities for power projection operations. Just as NATO earlier acquired AWACS, it is time to reconsider the feasibility of the Alliance owning JSTARS-like aircraft and even advanced ELINT aircraft. The discussions should also consider the costs and benefits of the Alliance's fielding of a deployable C⁴ISR system, battlespace management systems, and automated mission planning tools.

Develop a new allied deliberate planning model. The DCI will place new demands on NATO's deliberate planning process. Throughout its 50 years, most of NATO's deliberate planning has centered on requirements for collective self-defense under Article 5 of the Washington Treaty. The commitment inherent in Article 5 served as the mechanism for generating forces for NATO's defense. The DCI, with its emphasis on stability support operations, power projection, and a wider variety of operational tasks, must now be factored into the deliberate planning process. Specifically, the Alliance should reevaluate and adapt the current planning model so that NATO can plan effectively and generate adequate forces for the full range of contingencies it could confront in the post–Cold War strategic environment.

Under today's circumstances, the deliberate planning model should accomplish two important tasks. First, it should correctly anticipate the key defining characteristics of future contingencies—i.e., where they will take place and the size, modernity, and competence of the enemy. The United States and its NATO allies should conduct regular discussions to reach agreement on a typology of operations for future contingencies. Second, the deliberate planning model must include some mechanism with which to assure Alliance Commanders that member countries will provide the right size and mix of forces to execute NATO contingency plans in an actual emergency. This task is difficult in that most contingency operations will be mounted under Article 4 or 6 of the Washington Treaty, the domain of "coalitions of the willing." Nevertheless, it is imperative that NATO create planning and consultative structures and procedures to generate appropriate forces for its contingency plans; otherwise, the capabilities resulting from the DCI will fall short.

Consider a new category of forces. The Alliance should also consider the need for a new category of forces. Most recently, NATO members have conceived of their forces in terms of reaction forces, main defense forces, and augmentation forces, all of which were oriented toward collective (territorial) defense. As the threat to NATO territory has eroded, the number and availability of forces have declined, even among reaction forces. However, the Alliance's embrace of crisis management missions places new demands on prompt response forces that can operate far from home. Therefore, the Alliance should establish a new category of crisis management forces, under which each member, while reserving the decision to commit its forces until the actual event, would nevertheless prepare some air, land, and naval forces for prompt deployment and extended operations abroad. These crisis management forces might be regionally oriented or earmarked for a specific CJTF. The concept should be developed in concert with the allies. The objective, however, should be to get the allies to identify some of their forces for crisis management and to prepare them appropriately.

The discussion in Chapter Four underscores the utility of specialized European capabilities across the full spectrum of Gulf threat scenarios—in other words, in big wars as well as smaller-scale contingencies. It also suggests a sensible division of labor based on the principles of task specialization and complementarity that differentiates the specific political, military, fiscal, and geographic circumstances each country faces.

The inventory of allied "niche" capabilities sketched out below is not meant to be exhaustive. Rather, it is aimed at illustrating the scope of potential contributions allies could make that would generally not require large resource commitments or a politically difficult reordering of spending priorities:[6]

- The U.K. and France are the most outward-looking of the European allies. They are committed to projecting their influence and protecting their interests outside Europe. Both countries, in addition, have an expeditionary tradition as well as programs that are under way to improve their power projection capabilities. Accordingly, the United States should encourage London and Paris to invest heavily in RMA forces that are postured for expeditionary operations and capable of rapid deployment. These include strategic lift and other force mobility enhancements, projectable C^{4}ISR, improved logistics and support assets, and the capability to engage and destroy mobile ground forces (e.g., modern sensors, communications and control capabilities, and all-weather PGMs). The U.K. and France should also consider forward-based pre-positioning of essential support

---

[6]See Chapter Four of this study for a more comprehensive survey of allied "niche" capabilities.

items, which would improve their rapid deployment capabilities and strengthen deterrence by demonstrating broader Western commitment to Gulf security.

- The United States cannot count on the deployment of German combat forces in Gulf contingencies. Nonetheless, Germany could make significant contributions in transportation, combat support, and combat service support assets as long as the German government avoided slashing defense expenditures. Given the shortage of allied strategic lift, for example, Germany could be asked to assist in moving troops and materiel to the Gulf, perhaps by earmarking a portion of its long-range civilian air fleet. In addition, as noted in Chapter Four, Germany (and several other allies) could supply tactical reconnaissance and electronic warfare aircraft, which would help compensate for existing U.S. shortfalls in this area. Finally, Germany has substantial intratheater airlifters that could play an important role in enhancing force mobility.

- Many of the smaller members of NATO, including Belgium, Canada, the Netherlands, and Denmark, lack the resources to modernize and restructure their forces rapidly or extensively for power projection. However, they could contribute to other tasks in coalition operations. Some Dutch, Danish, and Belgian F-16s, for instance, have been modified for reconnaissance roles; taken together, the NATO allies have roughly 300 intratheater airlifters in their inventory. In addition, the Dutch, Danes, Belgians, Norwegians, and Canadians (as well as the British and Germans) maintain impressive mine warfare capabilities—assets that could be particularly useful for keeping ports, shipping lanes, and the Strait of Hormuz open to permit Western force deployments.

- Primarily because of their central geographic location, southern members of the Alliance—Spain, Portugal, Italy, Turkey, and Greece—would play a critical role in facilitating the deployment and sustainment of coalition forces in Gulf contingencies. Rather than encourage these countries to make RMA-type force improvements that are both unnecessary and expensive, the U.S. priority should be to ensure their approval for basing and overflight rights. In addition, and as previously noted, Italy could contribute tactical reconnaissance aircraft and intratheater airlift.

- The newest members of the Alliance should also be called on to contribute to coalition operations in the Gulf, as all are eager to demonstrate that they can produce security as well as consume it. While they face a large bill for military restructuring and tight budgets, for example, both Hungary and the Czech Republic possess credible NBC reconnaissance and decontamination capabilities—areas where both the United States and other allies are woefully underprepared.

This approach, of course, has its drawbacks. In particular, it could be seen as letting allies "off the hook" by urging them to concentrate on a narrow range of capabilities while eschewing responsibility for developing more complete power projection capabilities and air strike packages. There is some merit to this criticism. However, the benefits of task specialization clearly outweigh its drawbacks. First, it is politically sustainable, militarily feasible, and fiscally affordable. Second, it would demonstrate allied commitment to the principle of burden sharing. Third, it would inject greater realism and predictability into combined planning for coalition operations. Finally, it would produce important allied military contributions to Gulf security while averting the pitfalls associated with the more indiscriminate approach of pressing allies to build an RMA force or to participate in RMA combined operations.

NATO's implementation of the DCI and, more generally, the development of improved allied capabilities for the full spectrum of Alliance missions will be complicated in the future by the ESDP and, possibly, by growing European interest in missile defenses. Three interrelated challenges lie ahead.

First, the EU and NATO, as suggested in Chapter Three, will need to harmonize and coordinate their force planning so that forces developed to fulfill the EU's "headline goal" are compatible with DCI-related capabilities. For practical purposes, this means that EU force development will need to be done in a highly transparent manner and will have to be closely tied to NATO's force planning and review process. Likewise, it means that SHAPE will need to play a central role in coordinating EU and NATO force development and in planning for EU operations, especially with respect to EU use of NATO assets in crises that both organizations have decided should be handled by an EU-led force.

To date, speedy implementation of these so-called "Berlin Plus" arrangements has been hampered by organizational and coordination problems, leaving doubt in the minds of many EU countries as to whether the United States and NATO are serious about supporting an EU operation. This process needs to be accelerated and implemented in tandem with EU efforts to determine capabilities requirements, generate and apportion national forces to meet these requirements, and identify any shortfalls or overlaps that need to be eliminated. Unless the United States demonstrates a renewed commitment to "Berlin Plus," EU countries will feel a stronger temptation to develop military capabilities outside NATO, thereby weakening rather than strengthening NATO.[7]

Second, the EU will need to develop a concept for organizing its capabilities and structuring its rapid reaction force to eliminate unnecessary duplication and inefficient use of resources. This can best be done through expanded arrangements for pooling assets and task specialization. One potentially fruitful area for cooperation, for example, would be multinational integration of logistics support to circumvent the inefficiencies that typically result from national organization of logistics structures. This type of pooling may be particularly appropriate for some of the smaller NATO allies, which are well suited to low-intensity peacekeeping operations and face more serious budgetary constraints than larger NATO countries. Similarly, the U.K. and France, which have already launched efforts to improve power projection capabilities, should be encouraged not to divert resources from such programs to fund peacekeeping capabilities that could be provided by NATO countries that are far less likely to restructure their forces for long-range force projection.

Third, European allies, as well as NATO and the United States, will need to carefully consider the implications of European missile defenses for both the ESDP and the DCI. Europe will confront a serious dilemma in the future if it decides that it needs protection from the growing threat of long-range ballistic missiles in the hands of hostile

---

[7]For an excellent treatment of the choices and challenges the EU and NATO face in constructing an ESDI that is "separable but not separate" from NATO, see Kori Schake, Amaya Bloch-Laine, and Charles Grant, "Building a European Defense Capability," *Survival*, Vol. 41, No. 1, Spring 1999, pp. 20–40.

countries.[8] On the one hand, if America's European allies remain vulnerable to ballistic missile attack, they will be less likely to participate along with the United States in the defense of pro-Western countries that are threatened by regional aggressors. If this were to happen, Europe would become decoupled from the United States. On the other hand, there are simply not enough resources available for European countries to develop national missile defenses, implement the DCI, and realize the EU's defense ambitions.

There is no simple or single solution to resolve this problem, which can only be managed. The answer, although by no means neat, probably lies in some combination of bilateral, multilateral, and NATO-wide development of both theater and national missile defenses. Even then, European missile defense will be feasible only with improved transatlantic cooperation on defense industrial cooperation and greater U.S. sharing of sensitive technology with NATO countries. And even with the best of circumstances and intentions on both sides of the Atlantic, it is unlikely that Europe will be protected by a continent-wide missile defense system within the next decade. Instead, gaps will remain, but the goal should be to minimize these gaps and to ensure that countries that decide to remain vulnerable to ballistic missile threats contribute to the Alliance's counterproliferation posture in other ways while pulling their weight in meeting ESDP and DCI obligations.

 Finally, the gap between the United States and its European allies in power projection capabilities and military technologies raises the question of whether the USAF in particular, and the U.S. military in general, should make adjustments to accommodate allied forces. The preceding discussion suggests that the USAF does not need to make major changes in its plans, forces, or programs for air operations in a Persian Gulf MTW. That said, some modest adjustments in training, planning, exercises, and equipment procurement should be considered to maximize the effectiveness of allied contributions:[9]

---

[8]On this point, see Ivo H. Daalder and Philip H. Gordon, "Watch for Missile Defense to Become a European Conundrum," *International Herald Tribune,* February 23, 2000.

[9]See Peters and Deshong, *Out of Area or Out of Reach?*

- The USAF should use its military contacts with NATO members to develop and enforce common operational practices, standards, concepts, and terminology related to coalition warfare. Such discussions could also facilitate solutions to affordability issues and address other barriers to improving interoperability, including differing perspectives on doctrine, objectives, and operational tradeoffs.[10]

- Exercises should be designed, both within and outside the NATO framework, to identify and train for commonly executed functions, especially those related to allied power projection operations. One possibility would be to conduct regular CONUS-based exercises in which the United States moves European ground forces over long distances or supports the deployment of an allied AEF. If necessary, the cost of such exercises could be funded out of additional contributions by European allies to common NATO funding that supports the Alliance exercise program.

- An institutionalized planning process should be put in place to identify those allies that are prepared to contribute to air operations in a Persian Gulf MTW. Once these discussions have yielded a common understanding on the size, mix, and operational requirements of allied military contributions, the USAF should offer to assist these countries in developing appropriate plans and capabilities for deploying and supporting its forces.

- The USAF will need to pay much greater attention to the requirements for interoperability with allied air forces. Much of this effort should focus on reducing demands on interoperability. Such measures include avoiding mixed air squadrons; having the USAF perform time-urgent and/or data-rich tasks (e.g., suppressing pop-up SAMs/Scuds, C^4ISR integration, and air battle management); having allies attack only fixed or area targets and performing close air support only for their own ground forces; and scrubbing information exchange requirements. In parallel, the USAF will need to work the supply side of the interoperability equation. As it develops ISR systems, for

---

[10]While this discussion focuses on the USAF, the underlying principles apply as well to the other services and to the Joint Staff.

example, it should use standards that are accessible to those allies with which it is likely to operate in Gulf military contingencies. The USAF should also develop compatible secure communications, Identification Friend or Foe (IFF) systems, and security regimes as well as collaborate more closely with allies in ATO planning.

Since the disappearance of the Soviet threat, NATO has taken important strides in defining a new purpose that is relevant to the problems and challenges of the post–Cold War security environment. The Alliance's new Strategic Concept has affirmed that NATO will remain a European security organization, and its fundamental purpose will therefore be to extend security and stability in and around Europe to create a continent that is free, prosperous, peaceful, and democratic. The main threats to realizing this vision are instability and conflict on the Alliance's southeast periphery, especially the Balkans. Deterring these challenges will be NATO's core mission over the coming years, and fulfilling this role will require improving the Alliance's capabilities for crisis management, peacekeeping, and humanitarian operations. As such, the lion's share of the energies and resources of the Alliance, allied governments, and, to an increasing extent, the EU will be devoted to carrying out these formidable tasks. The process of NATO enlargement, which in the coming years is likely to encompass aspiring members in southeastern Europe, will also make a claim on the Alliance's energies.

Where does that leave the new NATO and America's European partners with respect to the defense of common interests against threats that lie beyond Europe, particularly the disruption of vital energy supplies? Clearly, this is a matter of a glass half empty or half full. Advocates of a more expansive purpose for NATO can take comfort in its perceptible shift in emphasis from the collective defense of Alliance territory to the defense of other common interests and values lying beyond Alliance territory. They should also be encouraged by the progress NATO has made in overhauling its outdated structures and forces and putting in place new arrangements and capabilities for new missions.

Still more important, stabilizing the Balkans, which are located at some distance from the main concentration of NATO's forces and facilities, will require improvements in the Alliance's power projection capabilities that could establish a better foundation for joint military action in high-intensity combat operations outside Europe if such a consensus were to emerge. Finally, Europe's growing determination to develop independent defense capabilities to cope with European security problems, if translated into specific resource commitments and military capabilities and linked closely to NATO organizations, bodes well for the health of the transatlantic relationship. Europe's excessive dependence on the United States, both politically and militarily, for dealing with crises in its own backyard is unsustainable over the long run. Together, all these developments are likely to lead to a more equitable distribution of the burdens and responsibilities for defending common interests.

Viewed from a somewhat different perspective, however, the glass remains half empty. While NATO is headed in the right direction, it has proceeded at a slow pace over the past decade, and progress over the coming years is likely to be uneven and fitful. Extending NATO's geographic and military commitments beyond Europe will remain highly controversial. Moreover, a huge gap is likely to persist between U.S. and European policies in the Gulf, notwithstanding their shared interest in preserving the unimpeded flow of oil. American and European policies often clash because of persistent disagreements over interests, threats to those interests, and the most appropriate response to those threats.[11] These differences are likely to fester for some time, precluding the necessary political consensus to underpin joint military actions.

To be sure, individual European allies—notably the U.K. and France—will make gradual improvements in their power projection capabilities and are likely to participate in coalition military operations in the Gulf on an ad hoc, case-by-case basis. Nonetheless, as this study has suggested, the United States will for the foreseeable future continue to shoulder most of the burden of defending common interests outside Europe against serious military threats, and thus America's search for a full European partner in the greater Middle East is likely to prove elusive.

---

[11]See Ivo Daalder, "NATO at 50: The Summit and Beyond," Brookings Policy Brief No. 48, Washington, D.C.: The Brookings Institution, April 1999.

Hence, if, after years of lip service, Europe is indeed serious about developing the capacity for autonomous military action in Europe while resisting military commitments and security responsibilities outside Europe, a de facto division of labor between the United States and Europe is likely to emerge in the years ahead: The ESDP will handle security threats in Europe at the low end of the threat spectrum, while the United States will do the heavy military lifting in Europe and play the role of global "security manager." This arrangement is incompatible with the fundamental principle of shared risks and responsibilities that underpins the cohesion of the Atlantic Alliance.

Therefore, the United States should reject this division of labor and continue to press its allies to shoulder a greater share of responsibility outside Europe as part of a new strategic bargain: That the United States remain engaged in European security and, in return, the Europeans do more to help the United States manage threats outside Europe. The alternative of perpetuating Europe's near-total dependence on the United States for meeting threats to Western security interests both inside and outside Europe will undermine the transatlantic relationship and could endanger America's continuing engagement in Europe, especially in light of broader political, economic, and demographic factors that are pulling Europe and America apart.[12]

---

[12]For a detailed treatment of these factors, see Stephen Walt, "The Ties That Fray: Why Europe and America Are Drifting Apart," *The National Interest*, No. 54, Winter 1998/99, pp. 3–11. For a more optimistic outlook on the future of U.S.-European relations, see Joseph F. Nye, Jr., "The U.S. and Europe: Continental Drift?" *International Affairs*, Vol. 76, 2000, pp. 51–59.

Adams, Gordon, "Shaping a Trans-Atlantic Defense Industry Agenda for 2001," *Defense News*, March 6, 2000.

Allied Forces South Public Information Office, "SFOR Air Component Fact Sheet," http://www.afsouth.nato.int/FACTSHEETS/SFORAir Component.htm.

"Armed Forces Employment 2020," Federal German Ministry of Defense, Armed Forces Staff VI/2, September 30, 1996, pp. 51–55.

Bacon, Kenneth R., and Thomas Wilson, DoD news briefing, April 30, 1999, reported at http://www.defenselink.mil/news/Apr1999/t04301999_t0430asd.html.

Barry, Charles, "NATO's Combined Joint Task Forces in Theory and Practice," *Survival*, Vol. 36, No. 3, Spring 1996, pp. 81–97.

Bender, Bryan, "DoD Leaders to Approve Revised Long-Term Vision," *Jane's Defence Weekly*, May 10, 2000.

Bonnart, Frederick, "U.S. Starts to Fret Over EU Military Independence," *International Herald Tribune*, May 24, 2000.

Bowman, Tom, "Shift Urged on U.S. Forces," *Baltimore Sun*, April 19, 2000.

Brown, Michael, "A Minimalist NATO," *Foreign Affairs*, Vol. 78, No. 3, May-June 1999, p. 210.

Buchan, David, "U.S. Urges NATO to Take On Wider Role," *Financial Times*, December 7, 1998.

Buncombe, Andrew, "Half of RAF's Warplanes Unfit to Fly," *London Independent*, July 24, 1998.

Byman, Daniel L., and Jerrold D. Green, *Political Violence and Stability in the States of the Northern Persian Gulf*, RAND, MR-1021-OSD, 1999.

Cohen, Roger, "A Policy Struggle Stirs Within NATO," *New York Times*, November 28, 1998.

Cohen, Roger, "Germans Plan to Trim Army and Rely Less on the Draft," *New York Times*, May 24, 2000.

Cohen, William S., prepared statement to the Senate Armed Services Committee hearing on operations in Kosovo, July 20, 1999, http://www.defenselink.mil/dodgc/lrs/docs/test07-20-99Cohen.html.

"Country Briefing—Germany: Fighters to Eat Up Most of the Budget," *Jane's Defence Weekly*, Vol. 32, No. 1, July 7, 1999.

Daalder, Ivo, "NATO at 50: The Summit and Beyond," Brookings Policy Brief No. 48, Washington, D.C.: The Brookings Institution, April 1999.

Daalder, Ivo H., and Philip H. Gordon, "Watch for Missile Defense to Become a European Conundrum," *International Herald Tribune*, February 23, 2000.

David, Steven R., "Saving America from the Coming Civil Wars," *Foreign Affairs*, Vol. 78, No. 1, January-February 1999.

Davis, Jacquelyn K., and Charles M. Perry, *Report on European Issues and Developments*, Cambridge, MA: National Security Planning Associates, October 1998.

Department of Defense, *Report on Allied Contributions to the Common Defense*, Washington, D.C., March 1998.

Drozdiak, William, "U.S. Tepid on European Defense Plan," *Washington Post*, March 7, 2000.

Drozdiak, William, "War Showed U.S.-Allied Inequality," *Washington Post*, June 28, 1999.

Ebel, Robert E., *Energy Choices in the Near Abroad: The Haves and the Have-Nots Face the Future,* Washington, D.C.: Center for Strategic and International Studies, April 1997.

Ebel, Robert E., "The National Security Implications of Oil," speech delivered to the Wilmington Club, Wilmington, DE, May 25, 1999.

Eisenstadt, Michael, *Iranian Military Power: Capabilities and Intentions,* Washington, D.C.: The Washington Institute for Near East Policy, 1996, p. xvii.

"European NATO Members Face Defense Budget Cuts, GAO Says," *Aerospace Daily,* July 30, 1999.

Fitchett, Joseph, "A More United Europe Worries About Globalizing NATO," *International Herald Tribune,* December 31, 1998.

Fitchett, Joseph, "EU Takes Steps to Create a Military Force Without Treading on NATO, *International Herald Tribune,* March 1, 2000.

Fitchett, Joseph, "European Combat Force Gets a Lift," *International Herald Tribune,* May 24, 2000.

Forsythe, Rosemarie, *The Politics of Oil in the Caucasus and Central Asia,* Adelphi Paper 300, Oxford: Oxford University Press, 1996.

Fulghum, David A., "Kosovo Conflict Spurred New Airborne Technology Use," *Aviation Week and Space Technology,* August 23, 1999.

Fulghum, David A., "Kosovo Report to Boost New JSF Jamming Role," *Aviation Week and Space Technology,* August 30, 1999.

Fuller, Graham, and Ian Lesser, "Persian Gulf Myths," *Foreign Affairs,* Vol. 76, No. 3, May-June 1997.

Fuller, Graham E., and Bruce Pirnie, *Iran: Destabilizing Potential in the Persian Gulf,* RAND, MR-793-OSD, 1996, pp. 71–74.

Gasteyger, Curt, "Riskante Dopplerweiterung," *Frankfurter Allgemeine Zeitung,* March 9, 1999.

Gompert, David C., Richard L. Kugler, and Martin C. Libicki, *Mind the Gap: Promoting a Transatlantic Revolution in Military Affairs*, Washington, D.C.: NDU Press, 1999.

Gompert, David C., and F. Stephen Larrabee (eds.), *America and Europe, A Partnership for a New Era*, New York: Cambridge University Press, 1997.

Gordon, Philip, *The Transatlantic Allies and the Changing Middle East*, Adelphi Paper 322, London: International Institute for Strategic Studies, September 1998.

Grossman, Elaine M., "CENTCOM Chief Rejects New Call to Cut Forces Patrolling Iraqi Skies," *Inside the Pentagon*, August 26, 1999.

Grossman, Marc, "The Future of the U.S.-Europe Relationship," speech delivered to the Houston World Affairs Council, October 1, 1998.

Heisbourg, François, "The United States, Europe, and Military Force Projection," in Robert D. Blackwill and Michael Sturmer (eds.), *Allies Divided*, Cambridge, MA: MIT Press, 1997.

Heisbourg, François, "New NATO, New Division of Labour," *International Spectator*, Vol. 34, No. 2, April-June 1999, pp. 63–72.

Henderson, Douglas, and Sir John Day, briefing, June 11, 1999, reported at http://www.mod.uk/news/kosovo/brief110699.htm.

Howe, Jonathan T., "NATO and the Gulf Crisis," *Survival*, Vol. 33, No. 3, May-June 1991, pp. 246–259.

Jaffe, Amy Myers, "Unlocking the Assets: Energy and the Future of Central Asia and the Caucasus," paper prepared for the James A. Baker III Institute for Public Policy, Rice University, April 1998.

Joffe, George, "The Euro-Mediterranean Partnership: Two Years After Barcelona," *Middle East Briefing*, No. 44, May 1998, p. 2.

Jordan, Bryant, "Overloaded," *Air Force Times*, August 30, 1999.

Kamp, Karl-Heinz, "A Global Role for NATO?" *The Washington Quarterly*, Vol. 22, No. 1, Winter 1999, pp. 7–11.

Killingsworth, P., Lionel Galway, Eiichi Kamiya, Brian Nichiporuk, Timothy L. Ramey, Robert S. Tripp, and James C. Wendt, *Flexbasing: Achieving Global Presence for Expeditionary Aerospace Forces*, RAND, MR-1113-AF, 2000.

Kittfield, James, "European Doughboys," *National Journal*, February 26, 2000.

Kupchan, Charles A., *The Persian Gulf and the West*, Boston, MA: Allen and Unwin, 1987.

Lesser, Ian, and Ashley Tellis, *Strategic Exposure: Proliferation Around the Mediterranean*, RAND, MR-742-A, 1996.

MacRae, Catherine, "DOD Reports on Progress of NATO's Defense Capabilities Initiative," *Inside the Pentagon*, March 16, 2000.

Menon, Rajan, "Treacherous Terrain: The Political and Security Dimensions of Energy Development in the Caspian Sea Zone," *National Bureau of Asian Research Analysis*, Vol. 9, No. 1, February 1998.

The Military Balance 1998/99, London: International Institute for Strategic Studies, 1998.

Ministère de la Défense, *Lessons from Kosovo: Analysis and References*, Paris, November 1999.

Myers, Stephen Lee, "G.I.'s to Quit Haiti; Reason Cited Is Budgetary," *New York Times*, August 26, 1999.

Myers, Stephen Lee, "Peace Strains the Army," *New York Times*, July 11, 1999.

"NATO Summit Press Release on the DCI," Washington, D.C., April 25, 1999.

"NATO's New Force Structures," NATO Basic Fact Sheet No. 5, Brussels, January 1996.

Nye, Joseph F., Jr., "The U.S. and Europe: Continental Drift?" *International Affairs,* Vol. 76, 2000, pp. 51–59.

"Operation Allied Force Fact Sheet," at http://www.defenselink.mil/specials/kosovo/index.html.

Owen, Robert C., et al., *Deliberate Force: A Case Study in Effective Air Campaigning,* Maxwell AFB, AL: School of Advanced Airpower Studies, June 1998.

Peters, John E., and Howard Deshong, *Out of Area or Out of Reach? European Military Support for Operations in Southwest Asia,* RAND, MR-629-OSD, 1995.

Pfaff, William, "Falling Out over European Defense," *International Herald Tribune,* April 13, 2000.

Piatt, Gregory, "NATO Adapts to Post–Cold War World," *European Stars and Stripes,* September 13, 1999.

Pickering, Thomas R., "The Transatlantic Partnership: A History of Defending Freedom; A Future for Extending It," speech delivered to the SACLANT Conference, Norfolk, VA, October 30, 1998.

Roberts, John, *Caspian Pipelines,* London: Royal Institute of International Affairs, 1996.

Rouleau, Eric, "America's Unyielding Policy Toward Iraq," *Foreign Affairs,* Vol. 14, No. 1, January-February 1998, pp. 59–72.

Ruseckas, Laurent, "Energy and Politics in Central Asia and the Caucasus," *National Bureau of Asian Research Analysis,* Vol. 1, No. 2, July 1998.

Scarborough, Rowan, "Record Deployments Take Toll on Military," *Washington Times,* March 28, 2000.

Schake, Kori, Amaya Bloch-Laine, and Charles Grant, "Building a European Defense Capability," *Survival,* Vol. 41, No. 1, Spring 1999, pp. 20–40.

"Scharping hat kein Geld mehr für neue Transportflugzeuge," *Frankfurter Allgemeine Zeitung,* June 26, 1999.

Skibitski, Peter, "Pentagon to Create Additional EA-6B Prowler Unit to Meet Demands," *Inside the Navy*, August 30, 1999.

Sokolsky, Richard, and Tanya Charlick-Paley, *NATO and Caspian Security: A Mission Too Far?* RAND, MR-1074-AF, 1999.

Squeo, Anne Marie, "U.S. and German Officials to Discuss Defense Deals," *Wall Street Journal*, August 24, 1999.

Stone, Andrea, "Panel Labels Two-War Strategy Outdated," *USA Today*, April 19, 2000.

Strategic Defence Review, "Future Military Capabilities," Supporting Essay Six, http://www.mod.uk/policy/sdr/essay06.htm.

Talbott, Strobe, "The New Europe and the New NATO," speech delivered to the German Society for Foreign Policy, Bonn, Germany, February 4, 1999.

U.S. Air Force, *Gulf War Air Power Survey*, Washington, D.C., 1993.

U.S. Air Force Scientific Advisory Board, *Report on United States Air Force Expeditionary Forces, Volume 1: Summary*, Washington, D.C., 1997.

U.S. General Accounting Office, *NATO: Implications of European Integration for Allies' Defense Spending*, GAO Report NSIAD-99-185, Washington, D.C., June 1999.

USNI Periscope Database, Nation's Armed Forces Database, September 7, 1997, http://www.periscope.ucg.com/.

USNI Periscope Database, Nation's Armed Forces Database, January 1, 1999, http://www.periscope.ucg.com/.

USNI Periscope Database, Nation's Armed Forces Database, February 1, 1999, http://www.periscope.ucg.com/.

Walt, Stephen, "The Ties That Fray: Why Europe and America Are Drifting Apart," *The National Interest*, No. 54, Winter 1998/99, pp. 3–11.

WEU Assembly, "Report on European Armed Forces," WEU Document 1468, June 12, 1995.

White, Bill, "Taking the Upper Hand on Oil Prices," *Washington Post,*
    March 30, 2000.